248.8

WILL THE REAL ME PLEASE STAND UP!

WILL THE REAL ME PLEASE STAND UP!

Lee Ezell

OLIVER NELSON

Thomas Nelson Publishers
Nashville • Atlanta • London • Vancouver

Published in Nashville, Tennessee, by Thomas Nelson, Inc., Publishers, and distributed in Canada by Word Communications, Ltd., Richmond, British Columbia.

Every effort has been made to contact the owners or owners' agents of copyrighted material for permission to use their material. If copyrighted material has been included without the correct copyright notice or without permission, due to error or failure to locate owners/agents or otherwise, we apologize for the error or omission and ask that the owner or owner's agent contact Oliver-Nelson and supply appropriate information. Correct information will be included in any reprinting.

POT-SHOTS cartoons appear by permission of the author, Ashleigh Brilliant, Santa Barbara, CA. All rights reserved.

Unless otherwise noted, the Bible version used in this publication is THE NEW KING JAMES VERSION. Copyright © 1979, 1980, 1982, 1990, Thomas Nelson, Inc., Publishers.

Scripture quotations marked TLB are taken from *The Living Bible*, copyright 1971 by Tyndale House Publishers, Wheaton, IL. Used by permission. Scripture quotations noted PHILLIPS are from J. B. Phillips: THE NEW TESTAMENT IN MODERN ENGLISH, Revised Edition. © J. B. Phillips, 1958, 1960, 1972. Used by permission of Macmillan Publishing Co., Inc.

Library of Congress Cataloging-in-Publication Data

Ezell, Lee.
    Will the real me please stand up! / Lee Ezell.
        p.   cm.
    ISBN 0-7852-8220-3
    1. Women—Religious life.   2. Personality—Religious aspects—Christianity.
I. Title.
BV4527.E95   1995
248.8'43—dc20

94-40801
CIP

To the recently recovered REAL ME!
Welcome back. . . . I've missed you.
God loves you, and (at last) so do I!

Contents

Acknowledgments

Thanks to Lela Gilbert for her help in polishing this manuscript, and for being such a "real" friend!

Introduction

Why would anyone have to write a book about a subject as simple as "be yourself"? It sounds more like a motto than a book. But I have discovered it is so important to give people permission to become their unadulterated selves!

It's a bit confusing. I know totally unspiritual people who have good self-images and Christian women who have very negative, self-defeating attitudes about themselves. How can this be? Personally, I know what it is to struggle with these questions. As a Christian woman, I knew intellectually that I was given "every spiritual blessing in Christ" and that Christ had given us "all things that pertain to life and godliness," but I still sensed quite a lack of life and godliness. That was a result of submerging and suppressing the real me.

If the issues of life (career, parenting, relationships) come out of the heart, as the Bible says, then we must examine our hearts. Like King David cried, we must also say, "Search me, and know my heart." If God will give us the desires of our hearts, how important to take these moments to regroup!

On the one hand, there are those who are asking, "How do I get closer to Christ?" Another crowd is asking, "How can I find meaning and purpose and feel good about myself?" Both questions are valid. The following is offered in an effort to strike a balance and have both needs satisfied along the journey to helping the real you stand up!

Identity Crisis: God's Lost and Found Department

Be who you IS. If you ain't who you IS, you IS who you AIN'T.

Baseball Hall of Famer
Satchel Paige

As I sat in the shopping mall, crowds of people passed me—people of every size, description, and style. I found myself wondering if what I saw on the outside genuinely represented what each person was like on the inside. What factors had influenced who they were? What hurts might have caused them to stuff the real person down and might have spawned the emergence of a false personality?

Suddenly a group of four giggly girls, all around age twelve, breezed by. I must admit I leaned in to overhear what the diverse group was discussing. The differences in their appearances were drastic, varying from grunge dressing to casual-hang-out-Saturday-shorts-and-T-shirt to Miss Prissy, perfectly groomed preteen. The girls spoke animatedly to each other, trying to decide in which direction they'd launch out to conquer the mall.

One girl was totally withdrawn and seemed content to do whatever the majority voted; if they'd just let her know the consensus, she'd conform. One looked distracted, brushing her hair, looking at her reflection in shop windows, concerned with whether or not she was appropriately dressed for cruising the boutiques. A third one contributed her opinion, displaying her fun-loving personality, pointing toward her direction of choice: fast food. The fourth was not interested in the vote but was insisting on having her organized way. She thought that was the most civilized way to tackle the mall.

In the end, the strongest and loudest girl prevailed, and the quartet awkwardly began to blaze the trail through the shopping center.

I couldn't help wondering to myself:

- *What factors made these girls respond as they did?*
- *Were they genuinely expressing or suppressing their opinions?*
- *Had someone/something thwarted their development?*
- *What influences had altered their true expressions?*
- *Which personalities were genuine? Which girls were pretending?*
- *Which of all the girls was the most authentic?*

This intriguing little pack of girls, making their giddy rounds in the mall, grow up to be us—women who shop in the malls, who sit in our churches, who act out our learned behavior as wives, businesswomen, and mothers. We are those grown-up girls who permit or disallow our true selves to emerge in our adult roles. I meet some real women, and I meet some plastic ones, fearful ones, and apathetic ones. Even women in leadership roles can be any combination of the above. Some are honestly playing out the person God designed them to be; others are just playing out a role.

False Self, Real Self?

In psychological circles, the idea of a false self takes on a more serious tone than that of style, mannerism, or social connections. Deeply damaged men and women, often victims of abuse, have a wounded inner core. They hide it from the world, and they may not even know about it themselves. They sometimes have puzzling dreams that give clues about their inner pain, and they may dramatically overreact for unexplainable reasons to circumstances that trigger some hidden wound.

Rather than explore the murky waters of the unconscious sea, those of us who have been abused or deeply wounded often develop a *coping self*—also known as a *false self*—which we use much like a disguise. Since we begin the development of this disguise when we are children, we become very proficient at hiding behind it and not allowing anyone—not even ourselves—to see the real, broken person who lives inside.

As I write about being real, I'm not trying to play therapist or attempting to help you with deep psychological trauma that may have occurred during your early years. I'm not suggesting that reading this book will help you deal with abuse or with repressed memories—that's a far different book from a completely different author. The need for that kind of in-depth help may even be a good reason for seeing a qualified Christian counselor.

What I'm talking about in the following pages are the conscious kinds of compromises we make, the everyday choices that we don't really like, the unflattering styles we reluctantly adopt. We aren't really ourselves because we're trying to avoid conflict, to please our peers, to pacify our spouses and friends, and to allow ourselves to "fit in."

Mirror, Mirror on the Wall

Women seem, in a sense, to be particularly vulnerable to this fitting-in mentality. By some mysterious process of osmosis, we've absorbed the mistaken idea that women are supposed to be able to handle anything and to juggle everything at the same time. A woman should be Holly Hobby Homemaker, but sensuous; be a model housekeeper, but hold down a modeling job; work full-time, but also go to school. Women are supposed to be dependent weaklings, and yet independent and strong when those traits are called for in the workplace. We're supposed to be the best-of-all-worlds women who can, as the jingle goes, "bring home the bacon 'n' fry it up in the pan."

The world has its own view of what comprises the "beautiful people." In reality, they are not necessarily the ones we might see on TV's "Lifestyles of the Rich and Famous." Greatness is not synonymous with rich and famous. There is Cher, and there is Ruth Graham, the wife of Billy Graham; there is Madonna, and in contrast, there is Mother Teresa. Which ones are really beautiful?

The world's definition of beautiful people has an entirely different basis from God's Word. God's definition of true beauty is described this way:

Your beauty should not be dependent on an elaborate
coiffure, or on the wearing of jewelry or fine clothes,
but on the inner personality (1 Pet. 3:3-4 PHILLIPS).

Dependent is the operative word here—our beauty
should not rely on outward appearance. The Bible verses
do not say that we shouldn't fix our hair or wear jewelry or
enjoy nice clothes. God knows as well as we do that if you
paint an old barn, it looks better! But God is encouraging
us to look within, to His original, more-than-adequate
creation, and to derive our satisfaction from a sense of innate
inner beauty.

Sometimes, in an attempt to be beautiful in the world's
eyes, Christian women make the mistake of creating an
outward appearance that is incompatible with the real self.
When I first met Tina, I was immediately put off. She was
seductively dressed—leather miniskirt and transparent
blouse. Her dramatic hairstyle and theatrical makeup
seemed to speak volumes about her moral values. But who
was the person under all that? I was taken aback to discover
a most conservative Christian woman who was sincerely in
search of God's best. Despite her foxy presentation, she
would have rebuffed any pass made at her. Tina's appearance betrayed the woman she really was.

I learned that she had developed her personal style as
a teenager in need of attention. She was a woman nearing
forty, but her fashion image hadn't changed. She was
misrepresenting herself without knowing it. You might
even say she was guilty of false advertising.

Unfortunately, a seductive appearance may very well
attract an abusive relationship, and a trashy appearance can

become a self-fulfilling prophecy. Women who dress like "bad girls" may be doomed to a string of bad relationships. All the while the genuine person is deep inside, hidden under all the Maybelline, screaming to be released.

The most beautiful people I've known in my life could never make it in a beauty contest. But the inner radiance of the life of Christ shining through a clear personality and a healthy self-image is unsurpassed by any dazzling outer beauty. It can shine through a person with a disability, through an elderly woman, through a child with a learning disability, or through a woman who lost her hair during chemotherapy treatments.

Identity by Label

The development of true beauty and true personal identity requires us to answer some strategic questions: Who am I? Where am I? Am I somebody? Too many of us don't really know who we are, but we are well aware of our labels. However, if we are able to describe ourselves only in terms of roles and duties, we are setting ourselves up for confusion since our roles in life can change all too quickly.

"I'm a purchasing agent" can be replaced by a computer.

"I'm a mom" will eventually experience an empty nest.

"I'm a corporate president" may find herself in charge of a bankrupt company.

"I'm a homemaker" could find herself thrust into the marketplace.

"I'm a hospital volunteer" might run out of free time.

"I'm a doctor's wife" may suddenly become "single mom."

"I'm a career woman" could marry and become a stepmother.

What you do doesn't describe who you are.

◆

Elizabeth had lived three lifetimes in her thirty-nine years, and she felt very lost. Initially, she had been a successful attorney with a beautiful office overlooking San Francisco. She got married, became a mother, and then divorced. Subsequently, she lost her entire business and was forced to file for bankruptcy. Elizabeth remarried, and she became a stepmother, attempting to blend the families. That marriage also ended in divorce, and by then a midlife identity crisis was in full swing.

Elizabeth had a number of personal problems, but she always identified herself by what she did. Every time she lost a role, she lost a part of herself. Only her personal faith allowed her to reconstruct "Elizabeth" as God's precious child, unique and valuable, no matter what she was involved in.

Big Shoes to Fill

I can relate to Elizabeth's plight. I worked as an executive secretary for many years, and I thoroughly enjoyed my career. Then I married a man who had been married twice but was never divorced. You guessed it—he was twice widowed, and I found myself tiptoeing around the memory of two saintly wives. Both of them were exemplary spouses and mothers. I felt as if I were walking in their angelic shadows, and I didn't fit the bill.

What contrasting families were merged on the day of my marriage to Hal! He was raised at a Communion table between services, while I was raised at a poker table between deals! We were such total opposites; our wedding invitation could well have read:

> *The Reverend and Mrs. H. Ezell*
> *invite you to the third wedding*
> *of their firstborn son,*
> *Hal, a successful businessman,*
> *to marry Lee,*
> *an old maid from Philadelphia*
> *who has potential*
> *but not much of a track record*

I felt so inadequate! To make matters worse, before long the reality of not being Cinderella set in, and I felt more like the wicked stepmother than anything else. My role in life had totally changed. I was married to a man who knew what a Mrs. Ezell should look like. He'd had two fine models and had been happy with them both. The reality dawned on me that I was to fit into the prescribed mold and fulfill the job description of my two predecessors who had done a great job. But alas! I was too round to fit that square mold, so I began to whittle myself down to size, trying to fit in.

I wrongly believed that I needed to carry on the previously set tradition of being a wife and mom in the

Ezell family. No one forced me into the mold. It was my choice to surrender my originality and attempt to play a role, like an understudy brought in to sub for two absent stars.

The difference between playacting and real life is that in real life, it's always opening night.
©1981, Ashleigh Brilliant

◆

Are You in a Role?

As a matter of fact, the theater was quite familiar to me. At one time in my life I had done some acting, and I had performed in many roles. I'd memorized a script and become the character, portraying that person as the director instructed. Sad to say, when Hal became my director, and the script didn't reflect my way of speaking, I didn't win any awards—no Tonys, no Oscars, nothing. Sorry, Will Shakespeare—all the world is *not* a stage, and we are more than merely players.

I play small roles in many people's lives, but in my own, I play the principal part.
©1981, Ashleigh Brilliant

◆

Many of us live life as if we were performing some prescribed role. We are directed by those around us who are judging whether or not we are in character. There is a certain stereotype for every position in life, and we seem to readily conform to the norm for roles such as these:

Pastor's wife	Schoolteacher
Nurse (not Ratched)	Therapist
Homemaker	Doctor's wife
Tennis pro	Executive
Retired person	Missionary
Social worker	Victim
Model	Chronically ill person

Do *you* fit the mold? Have you deserted the real you and chosen to conform to what others seem to dictate as being acceptable for someone at your stage in life? Are you "properly" conforming to the image required by your current role?

If we allow ourselves to be defined by the roles we play or by our relationships, we're setting ourselves up for a fall. Can you quickly list the labels by which you identify yourself?

_____

_____

_____

_____

_____

Do these labels portray you as you really are? Or do they simply describe what you do or the people you relate to? Many of these labels come with an invisible description of how someone wearing this label should look, think, and behave.

Are your labels keeping you from being who you really are? If so, find the courage to rip them off, so the real you can begin to stand up.

Real Men and Real Women?

Labels are ways in which we identify ourselves. Sometimes, however, the world tells us what we're supposed to be, providing labels of its own. How does our society arrive at its endless lists of stereotypes? More important, why do we try to accommodate them? I don't know. But quietly, subconsciously, these generalities exist and summon us to conform. And the stereotypes don't stop with women's roles, either. Nobody escapes the mold.

Real women . . .

are married with 2.5 children.
work and maintain a home.
have upward mobility.
use a glue gun.
handle stress with no problems.
work out at the gym.
can't fix cars.

Real men . . .

don't eat quiche.
watch sports on TV.

are adept at auto repairs.
don't cry.
never ask directions.
always know the right answers.
can lift or open anything.
are oversexed.

I feel sorry for guys who believe they are required to pull off the highway when the car makes an odd sound, open the hood, and stare knowingly into the cavity, even though they don't have the slightest idea what to do. Is mechanical ability built in to the chemistry of testosterone? Not necessarily. Does testosterone guarantee that a real man is rough cut, selfish, and sloppy and has B.O.? I don't think so.

In the sight of God, real men are not defined by how macho they are. Male identity does not automatically include having a selfish appetite, expressing a fat ego, smoking, getting drunk, or telling dirty jokes. God would describe a real man as one who fears the Lord, loves and honors his family, and acts with unselfish motives.

The Church Mold

Just as men and women are constantly subjected to stereotypes, false standards of behavior also exist in the church. Even in our religious settings where we should be learning about the real people God intended us to be, there are often little acceptance and encouragement for genuine expressions of individuality. The pressure is on to conform to the norm.

Although it is unspoken, most church members secretly hold a checklist for what their pastor should be like.

A real pastor . . .

has an uninterrupted daily quiet time.

would never have an answering machine.

can find Habakkuk without fumbling.

always witnesses to the person next to him on an airplane.

looks forward to hearing his home phone ring.

has read every book in his vast library.

remembers the names and faces of all regular attendees.

drives neither a pickup nor a Mercedes.

doesn't "ask for money"; he asks folks to "share their material blessings."

Likewise, there is an unspoken, acceptable pattern for the wife of a pastor, which I believe is one of God's most challenging life-roles. After meeting scores of pastors' wives, I sense they all feel the underlying pressure.

A real pastor's wife . . .

is a soprano.

plays piano by ear.

is outgoing, but not gushy.

is involved, but not interfering.

is devout, but not pious.

is attractive, but not trendy.

is the mother of exemplary children.

does not work outside her home.

How did these rigid standards get written into some subliminal law? Why didn't we get to vote on them? Although they are unrealistic, we mysteriously and secretly hold on to them. Consequently, our churches are full of stale stereotypes who need desperately to be told they have the freedom to express their individuality; it's legal with God!

Remember the funny character called the "Church Lady" who was portrayed in TV's old "Saturday Night Live"? Although the character was played by a man, she was quite a holier-than-thou, stereotypical biddy, hair in a bun, uptight about everything. She may have looked harmless, but beware—she goes to your church!

On the outside she looks like "Sweet Hour of Prayer," but on the inside she's more like "The Battle Hymn of the Republic"!

◆

Conform to the Norm?

Each year, my speaking opportunities take me into scores of church settings. These churches include Roman Catholic as well as every Protestant denomination. And in every church I find inauthentic people—folks who are hesitant to express their true selves, men and women who are reluctant to reveal who they genuinely are. They've sold out to some prescribed, officially sanctioned behavior.

Many women I meet don't feel comfortable expressing their individuality; they've somehow bought into the idea that they are meant to blend in, to adapt themselves to the mold of their church culture. They may be physically present, but the full expression of who they are is nowhere to be found. They seem to be holding back, insecure in the image they have of themselves.

I rejoice when I am in a church exhibiting diversity! When I see a multiracial setting, where people of all categories worship together, now *that's* real! I love to see an older woman sitting next to a punk rocker; a sophisticated three-piece-suit gentleman worshiping beside an outspoken, rehabilitated alcoholic. What a joy to see two women celebrating side by side—one overweight and overtired, and the other a bright-eyed, body-beautiful, aerobics instructor!

Bear in mind that this is not to say that the loud ones are real and the silent ones are unreal. The "real you" may be more of an introvert than an extrovert. She may prefer to wear more conservative clothes rather than more colorful, dramatic ones. But when a Christian woman truly feels satisfied with the woman God has created her to be, she demonstrates a sense of contentment and a willingness to be transparent to others, and she exudes authenticity.

You're the only one who can be you and get it right!

◆

Unreal Motherhood

Moms can also be victims of great expectations. So many false ideas exist about family bliss and parental responsibility. Where do we get fantasies about motherhood like this: "God couldn't be everywhere, so He created mothers"? It sounds warm and fuzzy, but it's untrue. God didn't create mothers as a substitute for Him! A real mom can't live up to such standards.

Real moms . . .

can solve any child's problem.
carpool.
have children who are their "pride and joy."
volunteer to chair the cookie drive.
don't blow their cool.
have homemade cookies and milk waiting after school.

I tried to offer some relief to guilt-ridden moms in my book *Pills for Parents in Pain*. I am a birth mom, a stepmom, and an adoptive mom. I know what it means to be a parent who cries, "Help! I'm suffering from a sexually transmitted disease . . . children!" But through my transitions of changing roles in my lifetime, I'm rediscovering the uniqueness that God handpicks for our individual personalities to pave the way for our freedom of expression.

Today, as I spend time with my now-grown-up kids, I still don't have all the answers. But I have a deep satisfaction and contentment with knowing and accepting the real

Lee. And I know that the more real I am, the more reality my daughters will be able to experience in their own lives.

Real-Self Reliance

Too many women have abandoned the provisions and empowerment God has implanted within them. Forsaking the resources He has placed inside them, they've relied solely on outsiders to meet their needs.

Even the best men God ever created are inadequate for the task of making us content or complete. Our satisfaction can't come from our position in life, our status, our labels, our roles, or our spouses. We've got to start cultivating the soil of our own lives to grow something that satisfies.

The Garden

After a while you learn
that love doesn't mean leaning,
and company doesn't mean security,
that kisses aren't contracts
and presents aren't promises.
And you begin to accept your defeats
with your head up and your eyes open,
with the grace of an adult,
not the grief of a child.
And you learn to build all your roads on today
because tomorrow's ground is too uncertain for plans.
And you begin to rely on the Son of God—
the Light in a dark world.
So plant your own garden,
and decorate your own soul,
instead of waiting for someone else
to bring you flowers!
Anonymous

It's cultivation time! Now is the time to use all the fertilizer that has been dumped on your life to grow roses! Unwrap that beautiful woman, and enjoy the fragrance of *you!*

Who Are You, Anyway?

2

What's all this about women seeking equality with men? I don't think women are willing to give up that much power!

Comedian Bob Hope

Who do you think of as a woman with power? Oprah? Margaret Thatcher? Obviously power, fame, and true greatness are not synonymous. Don't you wonder, really, who is the *real* Julia Child? She may be a gal who secretly hates to cook but is trapped in it. And when I think of Dr. Ruth, I can't help wondering, how can she really be a sex therapist? Now Elizabeth Taylor and Loni Anderson—they should be sex therapists—at least they look the part. I wonder what Mr. Dr. Ruth would say? And are there any baby Ruths?

The ideal of a role model—someone to admire and pattern your life after—seems a bit out of date today. Real heroes are hard to come by. Men are characterized on sitcoms as bungling idiots who sit glued to the TV, as super sci-fi heroes, or as absent males who deserted the family. The savvy woman of the nineties is portrayed as strong and independent, vying for position with men. Women on both the big and the small screens are depicted as promiscuous if they are feminine, and as high-achieving and ruthless if they aren't. Female role models are slim pickin's, too.

Linda talked with me while we waited in the beauty shop. She was low that day, and she heaped on me the details of her identity crisis. When her first marriage failed, she lost all confidence in her ability to choose men, and she fought the changes involved in being a single parent.

In her second marriage, she tried something new: her wrong interpretation of being a "submitted" wife. Like the women in the film *The Stepford Wives,* she smiled and subjected herself to all kinds of abuse; that hadn't worked, either.

Her live-in boyfriend had just moved out, and she described herself as "used merchandise." That day she was grasping at straws to discover who she really was and what she needed to do next.

Knowing and Liking Who You Are: Mission Impossible?

A popular song says, "I gotta be me—do it or die." Before we can be ourselves, we have to determine exactly who we are. And that begins with a positive picture of who we perceive ourselves to be. Let's work with this practical definition of self-image: self = your nature and character; image = likeness of an object as reflected in a mirror.

Self-image: the picture you hold in your mind of your individual qualities.

◆

Is the reflection you have of yourself in your mind's eye a positive one? Are you on the road to discovering God's purpose for your life? If instead you hold a negative picture, many damaging emotions come into play.

How Do You Picture Yourself?

	Impression	Feelings that follow
Negative Picture	I am unlovable.	Feels incompatible with loving, good associations. Wouldn't choose herself as a friend.
	I am incapable.	Feels inadequate; avoids any challenge; leads to inferior career choices and abusive alliances.
	I am unworthy.	Does not expect respect, and makes poor choices in relationships.
Positive Picture	I am lovable.	Decides she is accepted and wanted, and should be cherished.
	I am capable.	Has a sense of adequacy, that she does possess the raw material needed for success.
	I am worthy.	Has a healthy sense of worth that leads to positive companions and nourishing relationships.

I believe the negative view of self leads to a sense of a "Fraudulent You" while the positive picture reflects the real, God-made you! However, when we receive enough rejection to warrant withdrawal, self-hatred can take hold. We'll choose noninvasive friendships, never sharing below the surface. We do this on the assumption that if others "really knew me, they'd reject me."

Signs of Self-Image Problems

When a woman discovers the original personality traits God has designed for her, she will discover a balanced, contented individual. On the other hand, there are indicators—extremes of behavior—demonstrating that the real self has not yet been uncovered.

Unreal Signs

Aggression	Vs.	Doormat
Temper	Vs.	Placidness
Overachieving	Vs.	Unmotivated
Braggart	Vs.	Self-Belittler
Opinionated	Vs.	Convictionless
Overbearing	Vs.	Withdrawn
Perfectionist	Vs.	Sloppy

These extreme characteristics are not God-given in the original design; they are all excessive. And no matter what our undesirable traits may be, they are not something we simply have to live with. We have created and constructed our disagreeable qualities as protective coatings over past hurts and as reinforcements against the uncertainties of not knowing and accepting who we really are.

Are You Anybody?

Who are you *really*? I was recently at a very formal event, and I noticed that many of the people in attendance were posturing and posing, trying to overcome their insecurities. Although I wasn't exactly feeling at home there, I was doing my best to act at ease. Next thing I knew, someone bumped up next to me and asked, "Are you anybody?"

I quickly replied, "You betcha!"

Are you anybody? is an intimidating question of the nineties. It asks, "Do you have clout? Are you well connected? Are you popular?" Unfortunately, we're afraid to feel good about ourselves if we can't come up with an impressive, awe-inspiring answer to that often unspoken question: *Who* are you?

Where are you in life? is another toughie. This question seeks to determine whether or not you are successful (depending on what success means to the inquirer). It also asks if you've arrived at a comfortable, satisfying place in life. Not all of us can answer in a way that will delight our critics, but each of us should find a way of feeling good about where we currently find ourselves in life.

And as mentioned earlier, *What* are you? can be a major key to false self-identity, particularly for women. In the Bible, the apostle Paul taught that all of us are supposed to be all things to all people. But things are getting a bit ridiculous in today's world. In response to What are you? a woman is supposed to answer, "I'm an engineer," "I'm a nurse," "I'm an executive"—or to identify any impressive position with upward mobility as a proper answer. At the same time this career woman is supposed to stop at the market on the way home from work, cook a gourmet dinner and, dressed in a pale pink negligee, serve it with a homemade dessert by candlelight!

A greeting card I once received said it all. It depicted a typical American career woman, briefcase in hand, marching off to work. The text said, "Congratulations! You've finally become the person . . . your parents always wanted you to marry!"

Untrue Equations

Status + Recognition = Whole Person
Admiration + Appearance = Whole Person
Achievement + Performance = Whole Person

The more accurate standard by which to measure could be the following:

True Equation

You + God = Whole Person

More significant than the answers to who you are, where you are, or what you are is the one strategic question: Why are you here on Planet Earth? I believe that this is one of life's bottom-line, most important issues. And I hope, as we attempt to answer it in the following pages, you'll discover that it has a great deal to do with answering all the other questions as well.

Why Explore the Real You?

I laughed when I heard about a man who walked into a psychiatrist's office. The shrink told him he was suffering from a delusion.

"But I just can't stop thinking I'm a *dog*," complained the client, "and I'm driving my family crazy!"

"Well, then, this is serious. You had better lie down on my couch," advised the doctor.

"Sorry, Doc, but I'm not allowed up on the furniture."

Not appreciating who we are and what we are can get us into trouble! But self put-downs don't mean we are humble. Every now and then we hear someone sigh, "Oh, you know me. I'm always a day late and a dollar short! To be honest, I'm my own worst enemy."

Humility is not thinking less of yourself; it is thinking of yourself less!

◆

Positive self-image involves more than singing, "I wanna hold my hand." Of course, good self-esteem is not a magic elixir, powerful enough to cure everything from broken homes to poor management. But the human need for feeling good about who we are goes far beyond the ethereal, metaphysical subject of self-realization. It goes more deeply, spiritually, into certain needs our Creator has placed in our souls. A sense of belonging, of feeling worthy and competent, provides a basis for acceptance of ourselves.

> I say . . . to everyone who is among you, not to think of himself more highly than he ought to think, but to think soberly, as God has dealt to each one a measure of faith (Rom. 12:3).

Why Is Good Self-Esteem Important?

1. Self-satisfaction. When you feel contented with yourself, you are more free to care about others. You become less self-conscious. Remember, charity begins at home.

2. Freedom to love. It's difficult to fulfill the Lord Jesus' command to "love your neighbor as you love yourself" if you secretly believe the real you is worthy only of being ignored.

3. Sense of worth. When you feel unworthy, you may cheat yourself and, consequently, become stingy with others. When you're uncertain of yourself, you tend to feel competitive and critical of others. Self-acceptance releases the freedom to risk and offers the security of inner peace.

4. Springboard to growth. When you feel satisfied with who you are, you become convinced that you have the wherewithal to adjust, to grow, to improve! You're sure the raw material you have to build on is a good foundation.

5. Discovery of purpose in life. When you honor the Creator by believing He has fearfully and wonderfully designed you, you can more easily realize God's purpose for your existence. Sometimes you may automatically assume that what God wants you to do is far removed from what you enjoy doing. Not so! God's plan is custom-made to make the most of the real you.

God is all about disclosure. He has revealed Himself to us by taking on the form of a human, and He asks for us to reveal ourselves to Him in response. Naturally, there's no point in trying to hide anything from Him. He already knows far more about us than we know about ourselves. And as we open our hearts, souls, and minds to Him nakedly and openly—the good, the bad, and the ugly—we honor our Creator. His acceptance will lead to self-acceptance, and that in turn will release the freedom, security, and peace we so desperately need.

Is it possible that even the people who live with you have no knowledge of the real you?

◆

What Bothers You About You?

Speaking of the good, the bad, and the ugly, I don't know about you, but I've got some quirks that, at times, my husband and friends are unable to overlook. When they say, for example, "She's quite a talker," it may sound cute. But to be brutally honest, when I'm around, there are times when nobody can get a word in edgewise. I can easily become a compulsive gabber. Because I'm so socially oriented and I love to be with people, I enjoy talking. Even when I'm listening, I find my head preparing what I'm going to say next. This compulsive talker—real Lee—can be obnoxious and offensive. I tend to think out loud, and I am not even aware that I'm bugging the people around me. At times I don't try to restrain myself, monopolizing the conversation, dominating a meal out with friends, and being totally insensitive to the needs of others.

And talking isn't my only weakness.

Because I am a live-in-the-now person, I have a natural tendency to set my feelings by my outside circumstances. If the day is going well, if I don't have too many interruptions and things are going as I planned (and if it's a good hair day), I'm in a great mood. If the weather's good, I'm up. If it's lousy, I'm down (fortunately, I live in California!). If the music is upbeat, I'm joyful. If it's moody and sentimental, I feel lonely. Unless I remain aware of this totally undisciplined aspect of my emotions, I may easily ruin someone else's day besides my own.

Oh, and there's one more thing, too.

Hal calls it nesting. I call it fidgeting. Whatever it is, you don't want to sit next to me on a plane. I'm restless until I get my nest in place. After getting a pillow and a blanket, I try to tape the air vents shut so I won't get so cold. I get the barf bag out to use for trash. I ask for water, loosen my shoes, and pull out my briefcase, and at last I'm set for the trip.

This routine drives my husband crazy. He points out that most women just bring a magazine on the plane. But not Lee—no way! I guess it's because I spend so many hours 30,000 feet up in the air that I've learned to make myself at home in my plane seat. And I'm not naturally comfortable with flying anyway. After all, it's awfully *high* in a DC-10. And Jesus said "*Lo,* I'll be with you always."

These two examples just touch the surface of my multi-tude of idiosyncrasies, and I bet you have your own unique collection. By now we've realized the truth about each other: we are both good and bad. We all sin; we all make mistakes; we all have innate weaknesses. We must face our limitations, as well as our abilities, head-on. God could have just as easily made us without shortcomings, but He allowed them to be built into our temperaments, along with our strengths. These congenital liabilities remind us to depend on God, to humble ourselves, and to find compassion for others.

The real you . . .

gets discouraged.
makes mistakes.
has inadequacies/shortcomings.
is disappointed in others.
is not always God-conscious.
is not always honest.

If you were to be up front about the negatives you perceive in yourself, your list might contain some of the following:

Overtalkative	Procrastinating
Restless energy	Moody
Naive; gullible	Overly introspective
Undisciplined	Indecisive
Forgetful	Not self-starter
Impatient	Depressed

In 2 Corinthians 13:5, Paul encourages us to "examine yourselves." All the good, all the not-so-good, and all the lovely things about you need to be reexamined and re-aligned. In discovering the real you, you'll stumble across your weaknesses (if you are not already consciously aware of them). And because you're striving to live in reality, not just Pollyanna City, you want to realistically examine both your positives and your negatives.

Author Mary Ann Mayo writes that she was bothered because she didn't consider herself "fun." She wanted to be entertaining and witty like humorous author Barbara Johnson. Then a wise Christian friend reminded her that to have the spirit of Barbara, Mary Ann would also have to suffer through the pain Barbara has experienced in losing two sons, in coping with the homosexuality of another, and in nursing a husband back from a vegetative state.

"No thanks!" Mayo concluded. "I'll just be me."

Maybe you'd like to be funnier, more outgoing, and more gregarious, too. If you aren't the life of the party, you can make efforts to improve your social skills. You can work at seeing the humor in life. At the same time, appreciate your opposite strengths; you are no doubt supportive, encouraging, and sensitive toward people. Many outgoing people have to work on those quieter, more contemplative attributes.

What Pleases You About You?

Let's try an experiment. Make a list of your good qualities and call it "Things I Like About Myself." Your responses will speak volumes. Honestly list your assets—

physical, emotional, mental, and spiritual virtues. They may include the following:

Honesty	Good sense of humor
Open personality	Make friends easily
Sensitive	Leadership qualities
Compassionate	Hard to discourage
Faithful friend	Goal oriented
Love my kids	Good with accounting
Artistic	Detail conscious
Conscientious	Persistent
Open to change	Easygoing
Good under pressure	Good listener

Give it a try. Fill in some things for yourself. An analysis of the answers will reveal to what extent you are aware of the real you.

Things I Like About Myself

Put an attribute of the real you on each line. Think in terms of character, intellect, and creativity—both natural, physical, psychological, and spiritual attributes.

_____   _____

_____   _____

_____   _____

_____   _____

_____   _____

To Everything a Season

Before I knew who the real me was, it was hard for me to find anything when I went shopping. I'd have to take a friend along with me, someone to answer my endless questions as I tried on clothes: "Is this me? Does this look like me?" I had no idea of what "me" would look like if properly attired. I thought my best style was "25 percent off." I imagined my season must be "fall clearance." One color expert told me I was a definite Fall; another told me I was an unmistakable Winter. I became secretly fearful of being a closet transseasonal!

You can be real—even with a perm, contacts, makeup, acrylic nails, and support hose!

◆

How strange that the older we women get, the less of our outside appearance is real. We change our hair color, wear contact lenses, replace our teeth, coat our nails with acrylic, and jam ourselves into push-up bras. How odd that some personal vanities we once thought of as borderline sinful suddenly got saved when we got old enough to afford them. In fact, they are all legal if an original, authentic person is still alive and well on the inside—no matter what role she is fulfilling that day.

And that can mean anything. If you're anything like me, the real you plays many different parts in the drama of everyday life. I start out as the bleary-eyed, slow-moving wife. I'm the maid for a couple of hours. Then I'm a listening-ear friend on the phone—maybe even a counselor. Later, I'm Mom to help solve a serious problem. Or I may transform into Grandma the baby-sitter who makes funny noises. Still later in the day, I turn into a weary traveler, dragging my luggage through a crowded airport. When I arrive at my destination, I may be perceived as "God's woman of faith and power" by the host who picks me up. At my speaking engagement I'll alternate between good storyteller, minister, stagehand, and "Saint Lee." Then I'll return home to become the bill payer and trash putter outer. I'd go bananas if I tried to define myself by the roles I play.

And it doesn't help much more to try to find out who you are by analyzing, adapting, and adjusting your fashion appearance. Through all the phases of life, it helps to feel satisfied with whoever you see in your mirror. I'm not a very trendy dresser; even if I could afford to change my wardrobe yearly, I still don't think I'd do it. That wouldn't work for me. It's not my style.

Do you know what your unique style is?

Style is being yourself, but on purpose!
Raquel Welch

Once you reclaim the real you, your individual sense of style and personality will emanate from you quite naturally, although you may have to find enough confidence to demonstrate it rather than hide it. Are you playing it safe by attempting to blend in? Be yourself—and show it—on purpose.

One day, I dropped by a friend's home unexpectedly. I surprised her, and she obviously wasn't expecting anyone. Her hair was a wreck, and she had on an old T-shirt and a pair of torn jeans she couldn't quite zip up all the way.

"Well," she quipped, "this is the real me!" I was so tickled she felt free to joke about it.

Then later that same day, another friend, dressed to the teeth, drove by in a borrowed, red Mercedes convertible and called out, "Lee, *this* is the real me!"

Of course, you'll have to find some measure of balance, fashionwise. For example, if you think your style is a terry cloth robe and fuzzy slippers, you'll obviously want to modify that style for public appearances. But you can edit your look without pruning away the little idiosyncrasies that make you unique from everyone else at an event. You can define yourself without censoring yourself. In any case, you should do all this because it truly expresses you—not what others, or even significant others, want you to be.

Man Junkies

All too often women interpret who they are only in relationship to the males in their lives, whether that's a father, a boyfriend, or a spouse. Many women have no concept of their identity apart from a man. Relationships supersede self-perception, and male-dependent women cannot distinguish who they are apart from this I'm-incomplete-without-a-man-at-my-side concept.

Whenever a woman believes that she is not whole without a man, she may be prone to seek to marry someone who provides something she lacks—her "other half." She will base her relationship on the fantasy of meeting that imagined need rather than building a healthy, complementary relationship. This faulty sense of self-worth—based on feeling incomplete or inadequate—is one reason relationship addictions occur.

Some women become so strung out on their need for romance and the yearning to be with somebody, they fall into the category of love addicts. Being hooked on a man has the power to destroy a good marriage or to hold an abusive marriage together.

The stronger our sense of our unique value and worth, the less subject we women are to being controlled by our relationships. We must teach ourselves to believe that no human being has the power to validate us or complete us. That is an inside job. Tony Campolo, a provocative and entertaining speaker, tells of a husband who was about to leave his wife and three children. The husband told Tony, "I feel cramped. This marriage doesn't allow me to be all that I can be."

Tony wisely responded, alluding to a popular recruitment slogan for the military, "Do you want to be all that you can be? Then join the army!"

Me, Myself, and I

Although it shouldn't surprise me, I'm always amazed to discover how practical and applicable biblical principles are—even in these progressive years of the 1990s. The Bible admonishes against laying the weight of the self-image on our relationships or our roles in life. God's Word clearly counsels us to rely solely on who we are as individual people and to pursue the purpose and plan God has for us—the real us.

Verses in both Old and New Testaments remind us how important it is to understand self-reliance and to appropriate the Source of strength that resides within us— not outside us. Ecclesiastes 3:22 encourages us to concentrate on what we can do:

> So I perceived that nothing is better than that a man
> should rejoice in his own works, for that is his heritage.

Galatians 6:4 reflects God's desire for us to derive our sense of self-worth from ourselves, without relying on others:

> But let each one examine his own work, and then he
> will have rejoicing in himself alone, and not in another.

Where Is Superman?

Too many women have made the mistake of putting all their eggs into one basket—a man of choice—attempting to draw entire identity and hope from him. I speak as a happily married wife, but I know that my husband, as fine a man as he is, cannot supply everything I need for contentment. There is only one eternal Superman, and His name ain't Hal!

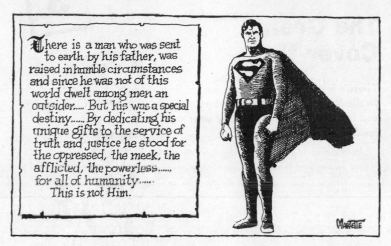

There is a man who was sent to earth by his father, was raised in humble circumstances and since he was not of this world dwelt among men an outsider..... But his was a special destiny...... By dedicating his unique gifts to the service of truth and justice he stood for the oppressed, the meek, the afflicted, the powerless...... for all of humanity...... This is not Him.

How true! Only one man has ever been able to fit this bill; His earthly name was Jesus Christ. And He is still the only One who can be all these things to all of us. And He is on our side! He is behind the scenes, cheering us on, enabling us to rediscover the women He created us to be. It's not going to be easy. It's not going to happen overnight. But with His help, we accept the challenge!

The Great Cover-Up

3

There's a period of life when we swallow a knowledge of ourselves and it becomes either good or sour inside.

— *Pearl Bailey*

T he story is told of Robert Redford being spotted in a hotel lobby by a devoted fan. As Redford stepped into the elevator and waited for the door to close, the female fan ran toward him and burst out, "Are you the *real* Robert Redford?" It was reported that, as the elevator doors closed between them, he replied, "Only when I'm alone."

Is alone the only time we're the real us? Are we ourselves only when the doors are closed and nobody else is around? I know that many of you live with someone who has no idea who the real you is. I've been that way, too, and in many ways it was my own fault. I'd never boldly taken the risk to let others know me; I'd never courageously unveiled my inner self. At times all of us have been careful to keep our masks in place, to continue the cover-up.

Many emotions—embarrassment, for instance—can cause us to quickly grab for some cover-up garment. Believe me, I know. My friend Alyson, who occasionally travels with me, has a great wardrobe (which I used to be able to fit into). One year, my husband and I were invited to a presidential Inaugural Ball in Washington, D.C., and I knew I'd have to raid Alyson's closet.

At the official ball, dozens of reporters circulated around, searching for tidbits for society page columns. One columnist from my local paper recognized me. "That's a beautiful sequined top," he commented as he approached me. "Where did you get it?"

"Where?" My throat felt a bit dry. "Oh, at Alyson's of Anaheim," I informed him, with a straight face. With that, I quickly made my way through the crowd and vanished before he could ask any more incriminating questions.

On such short notice, I couldn't calculate which would be less embarrassing to my husband: to read in the morning paper, "Lee Ezell was apparently tacky enough to admit she had borrowed her outfit from some girl-friend," or to read, as it was reported, "Lee Ezell was wearing a stunning sequined outfit from Alyson's of Anaheim."

Disclosing the Cover-Up

When we don't like what we see or we're afraid others won't approve, it's normal to hide or to cover it up. And when we are concealing something, we start posturing. Hence, the great cover-up is launched. Any number of negative factors can cause us to doubt who we are and to pretend we are something we are not. "Fake it till you make it" becomes our motto.

Concealing our genuine impressions leads to all kinds of hiding and game playing. And after many years of this practice, many men and women find they have lost their original sense of identity. This camouflage takes many forms, some of which are reflected in appearance—strivings to be counted among the beautiful people.

Body Image Cover-Up

The body is a sacred garment. It is the first and last garment; it is what you enter life in, and what you depart life with, and it should be treated with honor.

Martha Graham

You are *not* your body; you are just wearing it in this life—almost like a Halloween costume. Why can't we accept our bodies—warts and all—and move on to what's real? Generally speaking, many American women are too preoccupied with outward appearances.

- This skirt makes my hips look too big.
- This sweater makes me look lumpy.
- My love handles are showing.
- This turtleneck gives me a double chin.
- With these legs, I can't wear short skirts.
- My flabby arms dangling down look like flesh-colored drapery!

Don't try to be perfect: your imperfection is part of your uniqueness.

◆

We live in our bodies temporarily. Otherwise, how would we recognize each other? But the outside doesn't always clue us in to what's inside. In high school I would find myself drooling over some football player hunk, only to discover that he was a selfish, conceited snob. Then I'd wind up dating some twerp-looking guy and find he was beautiful on the inside.

How do your friends see you? Probably not as critically as you view yourself. Too often we are our own worst enemies because we're not friends with ourselves. If we treated our friends as critically as we treat ourselves, we'd be mighty lonely. Even the spouses of "ample" women aren't prone to complain; they usually moan, "Oh, you're making too big a deal out of it." Meanwhile our size 6 friends will complain about their "fat" thighs, and aerobic instructors worry over their bust size. It never ends. How tragic it is to encounter a woman caught in an eating disorder trap, with ribs showing through her starving body, describing herself as fat.

Happiness is not in getting what you want but in enjoying what you've got!

◆

Barbie dolls (those nasty little blonde hussies), television, movies, glamour and fashion magazines, and novels have given us the wrong impression. At my house, Barbie lives in the bottom of a closet with her boyfriend Ken (in sin?). Better this perfect duo never see the light of day again!

Through Barbie and other forms of media, the seeds of body discontent are sown early in the minds of kids. We've accepted the mythical concept of "change your body and change your life." All too many women, once they've lost their excess weight, are deeply disappointed to face the reality that nothing has really changed—except for their dress size.

What size am I? I don't know. I'm not in shape yet.

◆

Men don't seem to labor as much beneath these false body-size standards. That may be because men's power is derived more from their work than their appearance. If they feel successful, they are less uncomfortable about not being in shape.

When we women become more realistic, we will compare ourselves with real people—in the market or the park—rather than with the airbrushed photos in fashion magazines. If beauty *is* in the eye of the beholder, let's cleanse our viewpoint of ourselves and discover what we really need to be beautiful. In fact, let's stop comparing ourselves with others, period.

Perhaps one of the reasons *Phantom of the Opera* was such a smash hit was that so many of us relate to a character who wasn't as beautiful as he wanted to be. He was hiding his true identity behind a mask, and by the time he took it off, his rage over his inability to be what he wanted to be had ruined his one opportunity for happiness. As the song "Masquerade" says, "He has most to hide who never loved."

The Ageless Mary Magdalene

Use your imagination, along with your Bible, and consider this possible scenario.

She was a real looker. Everyone knew about her; gossip traveled fast in the little town of Bethlehem(?). Although she'd had many men, she refused to marry. Her hard life story was told in her eyes. Every man was a challenge to be conquered.

But when she met Jesus, she felt confusion she couldn't explain. He did move her deeply but in an unfamiliar way. Mary couldn't convince herself that Jesus was just another man. Before long, she declared Him to be her Savior, and her strange feelings of love were transformed into worship. Some believe that she was the one accused of wasting precious perfumed oil on Jesus. Certainly, she lavished her whole life on Him. Her love for Him was limitless.

The boldness of Mary Magdalene allowed her to be close to Christ in His life and in His death. She was the very first person to venture out to stand watch at Jesus' grave, only to discover that He had risen from the dead. Her courage put her among the handful of women who saw the resurrected Jesus in the Upper Room in Jerusalem. Ultimately, she heard His final instructions personally and experienced the thrill of watching Him ascend to heaven.

The real Mary Magdalene was not a hopeless, hardened adulteress. The real Mary was one born to give love, unashamedly. And her connection with Jesus brought out the purity of that heartfelt desire and transformed her life. Mary was literally brought out from under the covers!

Cover-Up Behaviors

When we forsake ourselves or turn from who we really are, we'll invariably begin to wear masks. Some common ones a real woman may hide behind include these:

MASK	MESSAGE
Independent woman	"I don't need a man!"
Cynic	"I don't believe a word of it!"
Withdrawn	"I'm painfully shy."
Overbearing	"I'm the greatest!"
Single swinger	"I'm not lonely; everybody wants me."
Pharisee Christian	"I'm more righteous than you."
Workaholic	"I don't need people; I have my work."
Too Tidy Heidi	"I'm perfect and meticulous."

Church Masks

It doesn't take long to discover that the church (like the world) has its own set of masks, along with an unwritten definition of what a good Christian really is. This unspoken standard is piled on the shoulders of any outsider who cares to enter in. And no two churches have quite the same unwritten code. For example, when I first went to church as a believer, I attended a Presbyterian one, and we had fun square dances. However, as I entered more typically evangelical circles, I was quickly told that dancing is frowned upon. For Baptists, raising hands while singing is strictly forbidden, but for charismatics, raising hands is standard operating procedure!

Prescribed religious roles are acted out in all kinds of churches, although I'm sure you know by now that being religious has little to do with being spiritual.

- In the liturgical church, the self appears pious.
- In the Orthodox church, the self is prone to conform.
- In the evangelical church, the self must seem humble.
- In the charismatic church, the self is zealous and expressive—and noisy!

But what reflects Christ? Each person, no matter what the church setting, needs to tune in to the mind of Christ for his or her individual action within that structure. Keep this in mind—if we *pretend* we have spirituality, we'll never get the real thing!

Christian women can sense the squeeze to conform.

A real Christian woman . . .

is happily married with perfect children.
has completed her education (but doesn't use it now).
only goes to G-rated movies.
doesn't laugh loudly.
enjoys long church meetings.
is present at Sunday A.M. and P.M. services.
prefers cooking a meal at home.
wears subtle clothing (lace collar preferable).

Why do these invisible pressures exist within the church? Newcomers are supposed to clean up their behavior and language instantly, gain a new set of friends, find an excuse to dump the old ones, and have a joyful attitude through it all. Meanwhile, these newcomers are expected to accept (without question) all sorts of eccentric Christian styles.

I remember having lunch with a fine young preacher and his wife. He seemed real enough. He had his feet on the ground, and he appeared to have a grip on practical Christianity and spirituality.

But when he stepped into the pulpit that night to preach, I couldn't believe he was the same man. He became so unreal! Instead of showing his vulnerableness, he pasted on a plastic smile, and he began speaking in other tongues. No, not a heavenly language, but one that sounded more Italian as he punctuated the end of every shouted phrase. It sounded something like this: "And God shall inhabit(ah) our praises(ah), and we shall (hallelujah) become(ah) the people of God(ah)!"

What had happened to the sweet, accessible, young preacher? Apparently, although his heart was sincere, he had developed a manner of preaching that he believed to be more spiritual than normal speech. What a transformation! I'll take the real guy any day.

It seems as if the church would like to schedule everyone for a delicate operation—a sort of cultural circumcision. Old frames of reference must be discarded, replaced by new ones. In the midst of this delicate operation, I'm afraid we lose many patients. Jesus told us that He came for the sick—not for the well. He came not for the ones who have it all together but for the ones who have tried to get it together and then couldn't lift it!

The world's standards of measuring up are all set up according to outside displays of success—wealth, power, clout, good looks, stylish clothing, and so forth. But because success as a Christian is based on what is going on *inside* a person, it can be more easily imitated. The depressed person can still put on a happy face. The pastor's wife can still appear supportive, although she's slowly dying inside. The secret alcoholic can still fill his seat at a prayer meeting. The disillusioned person can still say amen to a biblical truth he no longer believes.

How can we reach out to each other if we aren't courageous enough to let others see who we are and what we need? Maureen Kuehne, a woman who attended one of my Real You Seminars, wrote this poem for me. She calls it "Do I Resemble Myself?"

Do I Resemble Myself?

Do you know the woman who's called by my name?
Or whenever you look, am I always the same?
Either talking or laughing or acting just fine,
Not revealing the feelings that also are mine.

My smile and my face often cover the fact
That a joyful facade is quite often an act.
It covers the truth of the fear that's inside
As I swallow the hurt and replace it with pride.

But I'm willing to open my heart to a friend,
To show her the need that I have deep within;
To explore who I am, to learn to be free,
And ALIVE in the woman God planned me to be.

Elements Affecting Authenticity

Whether in church, school, or family of origin, any of life's experiences—positive or negative—can have the effect of granting or squelching freedom to the real you. For instance, early on in school, children whose last names begin with the letters A, B, or C may feel very special. They are always seated in the front of the classroom and find themselves at the front of the line. Alphabetical order affects them positively. But what about the X, Y, and Z children? Do they subconsciously accept the fact that they're always going to be last? Are they mistakenly getting the idea that their rightful turn comes after almost everybody else? Of course, it's rarely as simple as A-B-C. Following is a short list—an attempt to spark your thinking about other factors that may have affected the real you.

Factors That Contribute to Changing the Original You

Childhood abuse	Disappointments
Adolescent rejections	Failures
Victimization	Religious ideas
Physical defeats	Health problems
Career setbacks	Financial collapse
Marriage	Relational struggles
In-law pressures	Sexual shortcomings
Divorce	Prodigal children
Personal sin	Unfaithful friends

Digging at the Roots

A poor self-image is always based on false belief because God's Word tells us that we are "fearfully and wonderfully made." For an idea of how God views each of us, read all of Psalm 139. Further examination of some of the roots of the ugly tree of self-hatred will require more consideration. Ecclesiastes 3:1-2 advises, "To everything there is a season . . . a time to pluck what is planted." Let's take a look at some of the roots of self-hatred. Some of them may be similar to those listed above because damage to the real you often stems from self-hatred.

Roots of Damaged Self-Worth

Rejection, abandonment, and/or abuse
Difficulties with physical appearance

Harmful relationships (past and present)
Learning disabilities
Personal failures and/or losses
Unrealistic expectations
Financial struggles and/or failures
Unresolved guilt

It is the will of God that we be cut free of these harmful roots that are spoiling our growth and victory in Him. It is the Lord's desire that we grow to become "trees of righteousness, the planting of the LORD, that He may be glorified" (Isa. 61:3). He wants to make each of us into a healthy tree, planted by the rivers of Living Water, bringing forth fruit in its season. And the season for becoming the real you is now—no more cover-ups!

The Codependent Cover-Up

One major cover-up for past hurts is the mask of the caretaker. The seemingly Christian characteristic of helping others and not taking care of our own needs has gotten more women into trouble than we could ever imagine! While we were still seated on our brightly painted little Sunday school chairs, this codependent lifestyle was spiritualized and defined *JOY* as the acceptable priority for living: *Jesus, Others, You.*

Spiritually, that's the philosophy many of us were weaned on. And on the surface, it looks sweet and pious and righteous, right? Wrong! Because due to the unending line of human need, we never get to the you part. Furthermore, we often help people who really need to take the responsibility for their own lives. By rescuing them, we stunt them from growing into their healthy real selves.

Consider what the flight attendant says while giving emergency warning procedures: "If you are traveling with a small child, secure your oxygen mask first, and then assist the child." This is good advice for more than aircraft emergencies. If you are frantically helping others, you soon find you can't breathe. My advice is to take off the caretaker's mask and allow the real you to stand up. And as you grow stronger in yourself, you'll have more to offer people who genuinely need your help.

The Mask of Moses

Another popular mask is that of spiritual glory. One of my favorite Bible characters, Moses, was a living visual aid to demonstrate this particular masking problem. Moses may have thought he got away with it, but the apostle Paul pulled Moses' disguise off for our good!

Exodus 34 records the inspiring story of Moses on the mount, receiving instructions from God Almighty. Apparently, the first time he descended, the people physically saw the glory of God on the face of Moses (I think he looked a lot like Charlton Heston). But when the glory faded, Moses tried to fool the people, and the apostle Paul reveals his secret:

> Since we know that this new glory will never go away, we can preach with great boldness, and not as Moses did, who put a veil over his face so that the Israelites could not see the glory fade away (2 Cor. 3:12-13 TLB).

Songwriter John Fischer wrote a humorous song about Moses' experience in his thoughtful musical, *The New Covenant,* in which the character of Moses gives us some insight. Moses says, "Little did I know I was starting quite a trend; people have been veiling their inadequacies ever since. There are so many cover-ups in evangelical churches! If there were some way of making masks that would enable whoever wore one to look like a spiritual giant and somebody could market them in Christian bookstores across the country, they'd make a killing!" A song follows:

> "Evangelical Veil Productions";
> pick one up at quite a reduction,
> Got all kinds of shapes and sizes,
> introductory bonus prizes!
> Special quality—one-way see-through;
> you can see them, but they can't see you,
> never have to show yourself again!
> Just released? a Moses model—
> comes with a shine in a plastic bottle,
> makes you look like you've just seen the Lord!
> Just one daily application,
> and you'll fool the whole congregation!

> The New Covenant musical by John
> Fischer/Bud-John Songs, Lexicon.
> Used by permission. Music, 1975.

I don't know about you, but I'm not buying the Moses model. Let's remove the masks that hide our shortcomings and seeming failures. It is possible that if we persist in pretending to have such a precious commodity, we'll disqualify ourselves from receiving the true glory and revelation of God. We'll be left in the shadows, lacking the real radiance.

Get Out the Old; Ring in the New!

The old covenant Moses had to operate on was a stern one. There was only one known way to please God; the phrase "if you obey My laws and keep My commandments" is repeated over and over. There was no covenant of grace for them; they had religion the old-fashioned way: they earned it!

Thank God for a new covenant—one in which we can relax because of the grace of God:

> The days are coming, says the LORD, when I will make a new covenant with the [people]—not according to the covenant that I made with their fathers in the day when I took them by the hand to lead them out of the land of Egypt; because they did not continue in My covenant, and I disregarded them, says the LORD. For this is the covenant that I will make . . . I will put My laws in their mind and write them on their hearts; and I will be their God, and they shall be My people (Heb. 8:8-10).

If Moses were to speak out of the past to us today, he might speak enviously, "You are truly blessed. You don't have to hide because God knows you are not capable of keeping His laws on your own, anyway. You are much freer than we were to reveal our mistakes."

Shame on us if we hide our failures! We know Scripture admonishes us to "confess your trespasses to one another," but we've fallen into the trap of confessing only our successes.

Moses would tell us that the inner changes don't depend on us. We are insufficient in ourselves, but God has supplied us with His Spirit to put His desires in our minds and write them on our hearts. What a treasure in our earthen vessels! Sorry you could see only these "exceedingly great and precious promises," Moses; you had the shadow, but we got the substance! No more will we use our masks to hide our fears.

My friend Lela Gilbert shared with me a poem that she jotted in her journal:

Masks

Artful masks, so finely made,
Artful masks, so finely made,
Welcome to the masquerade!
Meet scowling Rage,
Prudence stern,
Logic, cold and taciturn,
Arrogance, and giddy Glee,
Leering Lewdness, Tragedy.
Strip them, damn them!
Look! See here?
Every one is hiding Fear!

Used by permission/Lela Gilbert, 1991.

Let the Unveiling Begin!

While we have the gift of life, it seems to me the only tragedy is to allow part of us to die—whether it is our spirit, our creativity, or our glorious uniqueness!

Comedian Gilda Radner

The "Star Trek" opening lines include, "To boldly go where no man has gone before." That's where you and I are, headed into the uncharted territory of life. We will be reclaiming our glorious uniqueness as the unveiling process commences. And it all begins with a commitment to honesty and vulnerability.

Sure, every one of us would like to appear wiser, more forgiving, more compassionate, and more motivated than we really are. It's quite natural to want to hide or disguise our weaknesses. But when we make hiding or blending in a way of life, we are fast becoming part of the chameleon population. Like color-transforming lizards, we're hard to put a finger on because we change to match our surroundings. We've learned how to fit in; we don't want to stand out. We must become bold to show our true colors and give others that same freedom.

Each of us is actually three people: the one we <u>want</u> people to think we are, the one we <u>really</u> are, and the one we <u>think</u> we are!

◆

Talk from the Heart

What does your heart tell you about yourself? If she is dissatisfied with herself, a woman may want to do some superficial alteration work, which can cause her to pay dearly.

Linda, who is slightly overweight, suffers socially because she avoids parties. She fears she'd be tempted by the food (or scoffed at by every size 7).

Wendy's career is hampered by her low sense of self-esteem. She shies away from jobs where she's forced into personal contact with strangers; she'll avoid risks.

Twila hasn't yet finished grieving over her divorce. She has assumed that the failure of her marriage was entirely her fault, and she has since plunged into depression and poor relationship choices.

The heart's self-philosophy will establish public behavior. Many of us have a mistaken view of ourselves, and it has acted almost as a self-fulfilling prophecy. If we think our usefulness is over, we make it so. If we feel sure no one will hire us, we don't bother looking for a job. It can sound like this:

- I'll never amount to anything. (Why try?)
- I guess I was born fat. (Why diet?)
- I can't pick good men. (Wait 'til you see this one!)
- My mother was right. (I'm a slob.)
- It's been downhill ever since. (So why look up?)

Proverbs tells us that as we think in our hearts, we are. What does your heart tell you about the real you? Your heart is the tablet God wants to write His message on—a message of grace and truth. The Bible offers us some sound advice with warnings about keeping a healthy heart:

> Keep your heart with all diligence (Prov. 4:23).

> Blessed are the pure in heart, for they shall see God (Matt. 5:8).

Could that be why we're not experiencing much of God? Because our heart-view has been distorted. Yet, even if the heart is sending us the wrong (negative) messages about ourselves from within, we can switch channels! The Lord offers us some encouragement about our disapproving heart-messages:

> For if our heart condemns us, God is greater than our heart (1 John 3:20).

Our loving God is on our side, to encourage us to accept His positive viewpoint of us:

> We are His workmanship, created in Christ Jesus for good works (Eph. 2:10).

The Self-Made Woman?

The finished product of a self-made woman is usually an example of poor workmanship.

◆

I wouldn't cherish being described as a self-made woman. I'd like to fully restore the originality built in by my Creator, the Mastercraftsman. It is impossible to reclaim our personal originality without assistance from the One who designed it (as impossible as making birth control retroactive!). If a building is leveled by a bomb, how can it be restored to its original beauty without consulting the original architect's blueprints?

To the degree that we rely totally on ourselves, depending on our own wisdom and psychological savvy, to that same degree divine help cannot operate. If a child stubbornly turns away, saying, "I'll do it myself," she (or he) cannot access our knowledge and assistance. But if that little one comes with outstretched hands, the broken toy (or broken emotion) is held out for Mom to fix. Mom's superior wisdom and experience will quickly heal the situation.

The same principle holds true with our broken real selves. By going to God and asking Him to reconstruct us according to His original intention, we have to stop saying, "I can do it without You!" Only then is He free to work.

A Little Child Shall Lead Them

Some of your original blueprint was obvious in your youngest years. Whatever happened to that playful little child you once were? Has she been squashed? Inhibited? Is she suppressed? Beginning to get in touch with your natural, enthusiastic self, and then giving that child permission to come out and play, will speed you along the path to restoration and give you a glimpse beyond the veil of adult sophistication.

Much has been made of the psychological "inner child." One interesting view of this concept has been expressed by Tom Jones, a chaplain at the York (Pennsylvania) Hospital. He wisely wrote,

> A little boy lives inside of me
>   who probably is a small-size clown.
> Is being grownup a time to put aside
>   the child who lives inside of me?
> Does growing up mean
>   killing the little boy inside of me?
> Now that I am a man,
>   it may be wise to put aside childish things,
> but don't ask me to put aside the little boy
>   who lives inside of me.
> I put him aside, to deny his right to
>   exist within me
> will mean to wake up one day
>   old, tired, and half dead.

I must be quick to add that there is a major difference between childishness and childlikeness. How does a little child naturally act? Uninhibited, impulsive, spontaneous.

Small children are natural born believers. And they'll try almost anything without a sense of embarrassment or fear.

Children don't think of themselves as victims, either, at least not until some adult tells them that's what they are. Kids take things at face value and make the best of them. We grown-ups could learn a lot from little boys and girls. In fact, the more difficult their lives have been, the more victorious they seem to be.

The Veil of the Victim

Another good example to us, when we're feeling victimized, is found in the Bible. The Old Testament heroine Abigail was a genuine victim. Her story (which begins in 1 Samuel 25) gives Abby every good excuse to go underground with the person she really was. By the time she was in her thirties, she had a string of disappointments behind her. Use your imagination as you read her story, and you'll see what I mean. When she was quite young, Abby's parents chose her husband-to-be, and at first he probably looked pretty good to her. Mr. Nabal was rich, and her family may not have been. Abby's folks assumed they were doing her a big favor; she would thank them someday.

But the Bible, which pulls no punches with its real-life characters, reveals that Abby quickly realized she was married to an abusive alcoholic. Fortunately, God's plan was to be fulfilled by the real Abigail—if she would not permit the unfairness of life to squelch her strength of spirit.

Although Abby was unschooled, she must have learned diplomacy by negotiating around the harsh moods of her husband. Instead of resenting his condition, she learned from it. One day, Abigail overheard that her husband had stubbornly refused to help the renegade David's men when they asked for assistance. When she realized the whole household was doomed to be wiped out for refusing to supply David's men with food, she made a decisive move.

Abigail may have felt ill-equipped in politics, but she recognized the right thing to do, and she trusted her natural instincts. She secretly rode off to intervene, disobeying her husband's wishes and granting David's request for supplies. By sneaking out enough provisions to assuage David's anger, she prevented a massacre. Abby faced David with raw courage and fortitude. She was no wimpy woman. She knew God's direction when her husband didn't have a clue!

Not only did David accept the courageous woman's provisions and turn back on his mission of revenge, but he later returned to request that the now-widowed Abigail consent to becoming his next wife. Now widowed? Yes. Because after she told her husband about her disobedience and how she'd gone behind his back to undo his arrogant refusal to help David, her husband Nabal keeled over with a stroke and died ten days later, quite literally shocked to death!

But even then things were not perfectly rosy for Mrs. Abigail David! Is her second marriage the happy ending? Not exactly. Abby became wife number two of David's three wives (kings were allowed such privileges in those days—talk about blended families!). And of course, there were the stepchildren to deal with. Later, when the camp was ambushed, Abigail became the leader of all the women held hostage. She could have won the Courageous

Women's Olympics gold medal for maintaining a positive attitude amidst the injustices of life!

But Abigail lived her life under the right assumption: God had given her strength of character and determination of will for a purpose. The real Abby boldly risked being herself. She was meant to be a lighthouse through many of the unfair storms of life; she refused to permit any wind of adversity to take her in a resentful direction.

The victim-you is from experience; the survivor-you is by design!

◆

Victims Victorious

Abigail had every reason to believe there was nothing worthwhile about her. She was a loser, and she had a track record to prove it. Since victims seem to inevitably feel guilty, she could easily have come to the erroneous conclusion that there was something bad about her. She must deserve the hard knocks life was dealing her.

But God had equipped her to be a survivor, a woman who had what it took to endure and even overcome injustices. You may say, "Yes, but I'm not a strong person like she was." Who says? Why would God have created some with stamina and shortchanged others? Would He purposely design some for failure and fashion others to be overcomers?

Not that Abigail couldn't have been tempted to think the wrong way. She was abused and mistreated—all without deserving it. She must have had plenty of reasons to feel sorry for herself. And any one of us would have sat down at a pity party with her. But she apparently realized that a self-pitying attitude would not help her and even had the potential to harm her further.

Just about every woman you meet could come to the same conclusion about her life. By the time we hit forty, most of us have had a few hard knocks along the way. But although (as Joseph put it) past experience may have been meant for evil, God meant it for our good. His specialty is in recycling the garbage of our lives when we expose the past to Him—the Light—and allow the unveiling to begin.

Let's refuse to allow our past victimizations to become shrines, only permitting them to be embalmed and cremated.

> **A victim is a yesterday person trying to get along with a today God who has great plans for tomorrow.**

◆

> Forgetting those things which are behind and reaching
> forward to those things which are ahead, I press toward
> the goal for the prize of the upward call of God in Christ
> Jesus (Phil. 3:13-14).

The Guilty Victim?

As bizarre as it may logically seem, victims often feel guilty. Typically, when a husband abuses his wife, she will feel guilty, filled with self-doubt and shame. The children set adrift by that situation will also feel guilty, assuming if they had been better children, Daddy would not have hit Mommy. Or gotten drunk. Or walked out.

This illogical sense of blame distresses its victims, causing them to develop a false belief system about themselves. This may cause them to try to conceal who they genuinely are and to hide behind a mask.

Unwrap Your Personality

Man's main task in life is to give birth to himself—to become what he potentially is. The most important product of his effort is the development of his own personality.
Erich Fromm

Work toward developing the uniqueness of your personality rather than just aggressively asserting your individuality. Amplifying your individuality could lead to haughty independence and self-sufficiency, apart from the need for relationship. And don't hide yourself under a veneer of shyness or timidity, either. Instead of playing these games, you are encouraged to enhance the expression of your personality, the uniqueness that God has given you. Allow Christ to emancipate your personality!

Don't mistake false humility for a personality; it is a crummy substitute!

◆

Many influences contribute to personality. In chapter 3, we discussed some of the negative factors from the past that affect it. But other elements make up your uniqueness. They include the following:

- Your nationality/heritage
- Geographical location where raised
- The family values of your family of origin
- Cultural influences
- Family traditions
- Your birth order
- Your parents' ages and social standing

The expression of the real you could vary a great deal if you grew up in Dallas instead of Budapest, or Hong Kong instead of New York City. If a woman lives alone in the Big Apple (NYC), she will need to develop some survival skills to coexist with the teeming thousands there. If she resides in a slower-paced society (as exemplified by many cities in the South), she may appear less assertive. If she lives in a struggling city in the Eastern bloc, the expression of her personality will be tempered by a totally different set of cultural influences.

In a similar sense, if your ethnic heritage is predominantly Latino, and you compare yourself with a British woman of the same age, you will have a different set of references for what is acceptable. But you should examine even these ingrained patterns from childhood to see if they fit in with who you are today.

Ask the Lord for restoration of the uniqueness He originally built into your personality and temperament. You're the only one who can be you and get it right! There is no one else waiting in the wings to be the real you. Don't let the world miss out on who you are.

The Lord, the liberator, wants to emancipate your personality!

◆

Life After Death?

Did you hear about the wife who quizzed her husband across the breakfast table, "If I died, would you remarry?"

Peeking over the top of the newspaper, the puzzled spouse responded, "What in the world are you talking about?"

"I'm just curious," she said. "Would you remarry?"

"This is ridiculous," he argued, but reluctantly replied he supposed he would remarry.

"Would you let her live in my house and use my furniture?" the wife pressed further.

Annoyed, he responded, "Okay, yes, I suppose I would."

"And would you let her use my golf clubs?"

"No," he answered from behind his paper, "she's left-handed."

Now that's what I call planning ahead!

What Is the Real You *Dying* to Do?

It is uncomfortable and may even seem a bit morbid for a wife to consider what she would do and how she would live if her spouse died. But it's worth considering this point because in doing so you may stumble into the question of "how much of who I am is wrapped up in him?"

A few close friends sat around the coffee table with us. "Hey, let's play," I said with an impish grin. "Let's all tell what we'd do if our spouses died, and the kids were all grown and gone."

Everyone groaned and giggled. One woman looked at me as if I had just taken out a large life insurance policy on Hal (I hadn't!). After some initial protests, we began to think beyond tragedy into different circumstances.

The responses were as varied and real as the women sitting there.

"I'd build an orphanage in Argentina."

"You'd find me in the inner city of Brooklyn, working with those kids to make a difference."

"You're all crazy to be talking like this; I won't play."

"I'd go to art school and explore my talent for oil painting."

I replied, "I'd be doing more of the same thing and scrambling financially to make a speaking and writing career, trying to minister to people."

The husbands looked at their wives in amazement. One man said, "Honey, why don't you go to art school now? Why are you waiting for me to die?"

Another said that was the first he'd heard of his wife's desire to work with children.

The question is, What are you waiting for? If you imagine you'd love to be doing something so different from what your marriage seemingly ties you down to now, why not begin opening the door to that possibility?

- If you'd like to become a serious artist, sign up for a class today.
- If your heart is in the inner-city problems, become better acquainted with those needs, and join some of the groups already in place to assist them.
- If you imagine you'd cruise the world, start saving for a weekend cruise this year. If your husband doesn't want to go, invite your friend (female, of course!).
- If you think you'd like to start working with children, train now by teaching a Sunday school class.

Now, answer the following questions as honestly as you can:

- How do you rate your energy level?
- What revitalizes you?
- What do you yearn for?
- What lights you up inside?
- Are you passionate about what you are doing now?
- If money were no object, what would you buy first?
- What step can you take today toward fulfilling that desire?
- If you had more spare time, what would you do with it?

Freedom is not the goal; but you need freedom before you can decide what the goal is!

©1981, Ashleigh Brilliant

◆

Can You Spare Some Spare Time?

When you have a few spare moments, what do you do? Do you read, garden, listen to music, go jogging, or putter? What are the luxuries you allow yourself? Now make a wish list. Write down ten things you'd like to do today that would give you pleasure. Consider these examples:

Play golf.
Go to an exhibition.
Hear a lecture.
Visit the library.
Walk on the beach.
Listen to music.
Make a special cake.
Start a novel.

See a movie.
Take time to paint.
Have lunch with a friend.
Dig in the garden.
Learn to dance.
Sew.

Don't put off the desires of your heart until "someday when I can be myself." That day has arrived. In fact, your "day" may already be half over. Today is the day! Get your imagination flying!

You have a magic carpet.
Your imagination can take you anywhere—
Maine, Spain, Iceland, Queensland.

You just tell it where.
So will you let it take you where you've never been before?
Or will you buy some drapes to match
and just use it on the floor?

Understanding What the Real You Needs

Because the tyranny of the urgent demands us to perform life's requirements, few of us take the time to analyze what we really *need* out of life. All we know is that we're not getting it (whatever *it* is). I'm not talking about basic needs, either, like food, water, shelter, and Liz Claiborne sportswear. I'm talking about personal needs that are uniquely ours.

Many years ago you could hear it glibly said, "A man needs to be admired, and a woman needs affection." That used to drive me crazy! I do think a man has a need to be admired—but he also has a need for affection. Likewise, a woman not only wants affection but also has a need to be admired, respected, and looked up to!

So begin a list of "what I *need* in my life," emotionally, relationally, artistically. Catalog the factors that are most important to make you feel secure and happy. Don't be shy! Include what you need to experience in your career, marriage, and interpersonal associations.

Your very personal list will not look like anyone else's! Each one of us has wants and needs that are innate to the real us. Are your needs being met? You must become consciously aware of them first. Your list may include such needs as these:

Sample Needs of the Real You

Recognition
Sexual fulfillment
Communication with _____
Adventure
Time for prayer and Bible study
Love
Financial stability
Variety
Respect
Quiet time for myself
To hear my spouse say, "I love you"

Be careful not to list any need that might fall in the I-need-to category. This is not a wish list of "I need to lose weight" or "I ought to begin exercising regularly." But if these ought-to's occur to you, they may stem from a need (I need to be pleased with the way I look). Often, when we face a genuine need that is important to us, it will lead us to action.

As I faced my list of needs, I realized that order was important for me to feel peaceful. Looking around my cluttered, piled-high office, I realized my authentic need for order was what bugged me about working at my desk. It was a disaster area, and I couldn't stand it any longer. I made it a priority to clean it up, and I tackled the piles of projects, correspondence, and photos that wanted albums.

Your needs may direct you toward your life's mission. As a person with a short attention span, I've always known that I need a very interesting speaker to hold my attention. Today I'm shocked to find that I am a speaker to thousands of people annually. (I feel like I'm living another life—a bit like Shirley MacLaine, except I have pictures!) When I'm speaking, I enjoy dressing up in something sophisticated and then doing some wacky, unpredictable things on stage. Changing the pace in my speaking, breaking it up for some laughter and tears, I'm keeping it interesting for the real Lee and, I hope, for my real audience as well!

I am better than I was but not quite so good as I was before I got worse!

◆

The Real Me Needs . . .

Write what the real you needs. Use a separate line for each need. Think in terms of emotional, relational, and artistic needs.

_____

_____

_____

_____

_____

Keep your list open, and as a genuine need occurs to you, add it. I encourage you to continue to explore what *you* like to do; consider it your private treasure hunt, leading you to a wealth of satisfaction.

Stripping and Refinishing

While I was rummaging around at a garage sale, my gaze lighted on an object in the corner of a cluttered garage. It was a small wooden child's chair, weathered and worn after years of use and abuse. It still bore the leftovers of many different colors of paint that had chipped and peeled; the chair was multicolored and unsightly. It had long ago lost its identity and value.

I imagined that, originally, the chair had been created by a carpenter to be a constant joy to some little child. But the old, battered chair appeared to have been painted a different color each time it was introduced to a new owner. It had come to its present state, hidden away in a dusty place—a useless piece of junk.

If you were to liken your life to some kind of chair, how would you see yourself?

A rocking chair?   An antique Windsor
A La-Z-Boy chair?   chair?
A throne?   An electric chair?
An overstuffed chair?

Are you new and shiny? Or like many of us who can relate to the old, beat-up chair, do you feel a little like used merchandise? It just might be that the experiences you've suffered have carved your chair into the unique piece of furniture it is today!

The Camouflaged Chairperson

Right there, in the middle of the garage sale, I could see myself reflected in that old chair. I suddenly realized that as I was growing up, I had learned how to camouflage myself so I wouldn't stand out. I can clearly recall that I painted myself a *tomboy* color because I was supposed to fulfill the role of being a son to please my dad. I learned how to be tough; I could beat up any kid on the school yard.

I well remember my mother's advice: "Look, sweetie, some people have beauty, and others have brains. Do you get my drift? You'd better learn to do something. Try to achieve." I obediently entered into the study of music and drama and tried to paint myself as a *colorful performer*. That wasn't far from being the real me, but I was still trying to create a different Lee from the one I lived with every day.

Later on when I got married, I quickly painted myself with *white lace,* trying to become a blushing bride. I tried my hand at being *domestic,* but it wasn't my gift. I noticed the folks who ate at my table tended to pray after they ate. For after-dinner mints, I served Tums. The best thing the real Lee makes for dinner is reservations!

Isn't this what we do? To appease others, to oblige, to fit in, we paint ourselves a suitable color for the occasion. I've met gals painted over as *supermom* or *student* or *Christian activist.* A shy person might be covering up with *alcohol*; a sexual victim with *promiscuity.* I run across women who wear a very thick veneer they call *independent woman* or *feminist,* as if this hard, protective coating can save them from further hurt.

Yes, many of us must 'fess up: we've painted ourselves a different color to fit into every period of our lives. Every time we've changed friends, areas, or spouses, we've added a coat of color. We've learned to imitate our friends, to talk about things that are acceptable, to own as many treasures as the neighbors, the Joneses. Many a woman has lost herself in the process and has wound up feeling painted into a corner. At forty-something the realization dawns on her: "Somewhere along the line I've forgotten my true identity; I don't know who I am!"

Restoring the Original You

What a lesson I was to learn as I began stripping that battered old child's chair! Underneath all the paint colors and chipped veneers, I discovered the wood was solid oak. No one could have imagined it was valuable. The lovely grain of the wood and its rich shading had long ago been coated over and over with cheap, imitation colors.

I believe God wants us to strip off those layers covering up the intrinsic value of His original creation. Then folks can see—clearly and obviously—who we really are. And you've got the Manufacturer's guarantee: underneath it all is a true beauty—the real you.

Christian Strippers, Unite!

Let's agree to not fake it anymore. Dedicate yourself to the task of stripping off all outer camouflage, unmasking the genuine article. Make this commitment:

God made me a certain special way. I'm going to make myself vulnerable. I'm going to become a Christian stripper— ruthlessly dedicated to the task of getting rid of all coatings of pretense.

◆

Now let's pray this prayer together:

O God, I feel the person I seem to be right now may not really be the real me—the person You originally had in mind.

Jesus, You know I've made some wrong choices and chosen some dark paths that have brought me to where I am today.

I don't want to lose sight of the beautiful person You intended me to become.

If I've misinterpreted Your signals, if I've misused Your gifts, please forgive me.

I desire restoration, to know the truth, and to be conformed to Your original plan.

Give me eyes to see that plan, ears to hear Your voice, and the courage to become the real me!

In the name of Jesus Christ. Amen.

Step No. 1: Receive the Truth

You shall know the truth, and the truth shall make you free. . . . Therefore if the Son makes you free, you shall be free indeed.

Jesus

Did you know the real you has a hollow, empty place deep inside? That emptiness was designed to remain unfilled until you establish a relationship with Jesus Christ by inviting Him into your life. Some refer to this space as the *God void*. Whatever you choose to call it, that inner emptiness is a real part of you that is incomplete without His presence. Folks try to stuff all kinds of substitutes into this space—material goods, relationships, careers, alcohol, food, drugs, and countless other substitutes—but the emptiness within people is reserved for God and His truth.

We can't do a better job of being ourselves by trying harder. Pulling ourselves up by our bootstraps won't cut it; we'd be working against gravity. We must have our grip firmly placed on some solid object above ourselves in order to be hoisted up higher. I believe that firm support is Jesus—"the Rock that is higher than I."

The book of Proverbs encourages us to "buy the truth, and do not sell it" (23:23)! Many of us have sold our authenticity; worse yet, some of us have given it away. But if we buy the scriptural truth about ourselves, we'll have a solid foundation to build our lives on. Pilate asked Jesus, "What is truth?" We might well ask that question ourselves. One thing is clear: the greatest truth you can discover is what God says about you. And even when you feel that God has abandoned you, God's truth assures you: "I still love you; I will never leave you or forsake you."

Jesus said, "I am the way, the truth, and the life." When we miss sleep, have a grave disappointment, or take in too much sugar, our emotions may tell us something contrary. But the truth is that we are "the apple of God's eye." When our topsy-turvy emotions tell us we are nobodies, the truth about us is that we are made "in the image of God." That doesn't sound like people created to fail or things to discard!

When we feel that we're worthless, the truth is, we have been "bought at a price"—and that price was the death of Jesus, God's only Son. If God thought we were worth purchasing through the agony of His Son's death, we should respect ourselves accordingly. And when it seems hard to accept ourselves as we are, we ought to remind ourselves of another truth: we are "hidden with Christ in God"; we are "accepted in the Beloved."

The Truth of Why You're Here!

Did you realize that before you were a gleam in your parents' eyes, you were God's idea? That is some of the great truth about you. Your parents didn't decide to make *you*; they just decided to make love. God is the One who decided to make you! This truth is confirmed over and over again in Scriptures like this one, as King David spoke to God, saying,

> You made all the delicate, inner parts of my body, and knit them together in my mother's womb. . . . You were there while I was being formed in utter seclusion! You saw me before I was born (Ps. 139:13–16 TLB).

What a comfort it was for me to uncover this truth in the Bible! I was one of five daughters born to a father who exclusively wanted a son; that's why my name isn't spelled something feminine like Leigh. Although I may have been unwanted by my parents, my heavenly Father planned my existence for me without their consent.

The act of love was your parents' decision; the act of life was God's decision.

◆

A redheaded adoptee shyly remarked to me, "I'm an unwanted child, born out of wedlock, and I don't know who my father is." Everything in me was overjoyed to inform her, "Impossible! There is no such thing as an 'illegitimate' child. I can assure you that, bottom line, we both share the same Father. God is our Father. Even though my parents were married, they didn't volunteer for me, either!"

The young woman broke into tears.

"Maybe that's why," I comforted her, "Jesus advised us to 'call no one father except your Father in heaven.' That makes us both legit!"

Think back to the night you were conceived—way back there. How do you imagine it was? Do you think your daddy probably looked at your mom with a gleam in his eye and, winking, said, "Hey, honey, let's go upstairs and make a little Casey tonight." Not! I doubt that dude was thinking about baby Casey at all. But Someone with more power and wisdom than Mom and Dad was thinking about Casey and thinking about her in great love.

The conception of any child was God's idea first. He never consulted with our parents to see if it was a convenient time for them, or if they lived in the right place or were financially secure enough, or if the child would fit into their long-range plans. He had a plan that superseded theirs. Five billion sperm were swimming around in there, and guess what? You won!

Special Ordinary People

Even the folks God used in a great way, whose lives are recorded in the Scriptures, weren't superpowers. They all seemed a bit hesitant about whether they were fully equipped for the job God called them to, but they had to be real.

Why did God choose little Mary to give birth to His Son? Because even as a teenager, she was vulnerable and real, and she didn't mind showing it. When the angel appeared to her, she let him know she was scared stiff. That's why the angel's first words were, "Do not be afraid, Mary, for you have found favor with God." And after the angelic being announced that she would soon be pregnant, she questioned him with genuine honesty and uncertainty, saying, "How can this be?"

As she humbly accepted God's will, she could surrender by saying, "Let it be to me according to your word." Surrender was easy for Mary; she knew the God she was dealing with was real. Then, like the genuinely confused teenager she was, Mary ran to a friend for reassurance, her cousin Elizabeth. Every one of us needs someone we can be real with. Even the Blessed Virgin ran to her friend and relative Elizabeth to spill the beans about what was happening to the real Mary!

Telling Joseph must have been very uncomfortable for her. Hers would sound like a "likely" story to any fiancé who had not sexually given in to his loving impulses. Mary knew she was risking Joseph's breaking the engagement. In fact, it took another angelic intervention to convince Joseph otherwise. Then, after the baby Jesus came, wise Simeon prepared Mary for further struggles:

> A sword shall pierce your soul, for this child shall be rejected by many. . . . And the deepest thoughts of many hearts shall be revealed (Luke 2:34 TLB).

Mary was finally getting the picture: she wouldn't appear to be blessed, yet she knew someday "all generations will call me blessed." God knew the Mary-and-Joseph wedding wouldn't be all that joyful to the bride's and groom's parents—they knew the young woman was already pregnant. And even though Mary's story of becoming pregnant through a divine encounter was true, you have to wonder how many people actually bought it.

Despite all this, God knew Mary had what it would take to courageously confront all the difficulties Jesus' birth would bring into her life. One reason He could count on her was that she was real. Mary could hold her head high amidst misunderstanding and accusation. She was not the kind to lie about her wedding anniversary, even though her son Jesus' age didn't add up. The whispered scorn and gossip about her "illegitimate" son probably continued for years. (I'm sure they had their own *Jerusalem Enquirer* system of spreading gossip.)

Even Jesus Himself offered challenges to her. But instead of being insulted by His remark about her— "Woman, what have I to do with you?"—the real Mary advised the doubting crowd, "Whatever Jesus says to you, do it." Finally, because she had been authentic throughout Jesus' thirty years on earth, Mary could risk being seen at the cross, and she even found the courage to believe the good news that He had been resurrected.

Real Heroes

Mary wasn't the only person who felt inadequate when God called. The powerful prophet Jeremiah responded, "I cannot speak, for I am a child." God gently reminded Jeremiah that his Creator was well aware of Jeremiah's qualities by saying, "Before I formed you in the womb I knew you."

When an angel of the Lord called Gideon out from his hiding place, he was greeted with "The LORD is with you, you mighty man of valor!" Gideon began his objections, trying desperately to convince the angel that he must have the wrong man.

When God called Moses to be His spokesman, although he was a highly educated man, he objected, "I am not eloquent . . . I am slow of speech" (Exod. 4:10). It was obvious that Moses was the appropriate person for the task. Moses was a prince in Egypt, but he was acting like a pitiful slave of Egypt, inadequate for a meaningful assignment. God wouldn't accept Moses' excuses; the Creator had too much invested in His reluctant servant.

As our faith increases, we also increase our sense of value. Romans 12:3 tells us, "Be honest in your estimate of yourselves, measuring your value by how much faith God has given you" (TLB). This implies that we can conclude only that we are significant to God once we understand the high price Jesus paid for us.

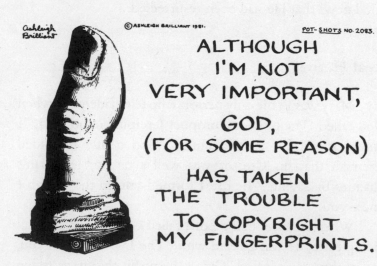

Ashleigh Brilliant

©ASHLEIGH BRILLIANT 1981.

POT-SHOTS NO. 2093.

ALTHOUGH I'M NOT VERY IMPORTANT, GOD, (FOR SOME REASON) HAS TAKEN THE TROUBLE TO COPYRIGHT MY FINGERPRINTS.

God Loves You Unconditionally

It is so hard for us humans to grasp God's truth about us—it goes against our nature. But God decided, long before we were born, that He would demonstrate His *un*conditional love for us by sending His own Son, Jesus, to pay the penalty of death for our sins. God's decision to love us occurred long before we did anything to deserve it. Thank God, He doesn't give us what we deserve; He gives us what we need. Someone put it:

God loves you whether you are in a state of grace or disgrace.

◆

Even if you feel dead to the possibility of God's renewal in your life, I believe in that possibility because of verses like Ephesians 2:4-5:

> But God is so rich in mercy . . . that even though we
> were spiritually dead and doomed by our sins, he gave us
> back our lives again when he raised Christ from the dead
> (TLB).

Christ didn't die on the cross for beings of little or no value. God didn't waste Jesus in death for some species not much better than the animals! Because God's creation in us human beings was so perfect and had such potential, He wants us to reach that potential. We can be sure God didn't create us to be the piece of junk we may feel we are. Instead, He is willing to help us recycle the garbage in our lives.

There is no magic, but the woman who knows Jesus has not only a greater opportunity for a better self-image but also the means to develop herself to the fullest.

◆

Too many gals seem to think that to fulfill God's desires for them, they'll have to become something they are not. But the Bible clearly describes our born-again experience not merely as getting our heavenly insurance policy but actually as becoming women we never had the power to transform into before—conforming to our original design.

Why Be the Role Model for a Stereotype?

Our uniqueness makes us very valuable. In a Yale University study, one chemical biologist calculated our physical components alone are extravagantly precious. When you add up the value of the enzymes, hormones, organs, and muscles in the average-sized adult, each of us is worth $6,000,015.44. Imagine—each female human being is a six-million-dollar woman!

Beyond your chemical composition, you were wired in a special, unusual way for a specific purpose God had in mind for you. Then He laced your temperament together with certain matching gifts and talents, all intended to work together toward the fulfillment of your life and His plan.

Your uniqueness is expressed in much more than your fingerprints. The entire structure of your nature, character, temperament, and personality is custom-designed. You are God's way of being creative!

> **You are one of a kind. In other words, when God made you, He said, "I'll never do THAT again!"**

◆

Recognizing this truth and reconciling yourself to it will supply you the needed courage for further self-examination. You can know for sure, in this stripping process of putting off the old you and putting on the new woman, you will not be disappointed in what you find under it all. For one thing, your original creation is much more resilient and pleasing than the one you may be acquainted with now. You'll find a person you can be proud of. The real you is the woman in whom God has invested all this uniqueness and value—the one He wants to use for His purposes.

No *Real* Alternative Lifestyle

We can be pleased and confident in expressing ourselves the way God created us. When it comes to the real us, we have nothing to be ashamed of. God has not created us to be embarrassments to Him or to ourselves. For instance, God never created anyone to be a homosexual; the Bible is clear that this "alternative lifestyle" is in complete opposition to the will of God.

Two friends of mine, Robert and Jerry, were converted to Christ out of the gay community. They both embraced His love, and they taught me a lot about their former homosexual orientation. Both men confessed to using the God-made-me-this-way excuse to support their chosen behavior, while they knew in their hearts that God had not originally designed them to live as they did.

Like many homosexuals, both men had become convinced, through experiencing a childhood sexual assault, that there was something odd about them. The scenarios began to build up from the time of the assault, and both men, believing a tragic lie about themselves, chose to withdraw from the nongay community and to demonstrate gay dress and mannerisms. The rest is history.

I journeyed with both men to the bitter end. Although each of them repented and converted to Christianity, both died gruesome deaths from AIDS. You can be sure God never designed any one of us to be doomed to die in such a manner.

God Cared Enough to Send the Very Best

Because we are so valuable in God's eyes, He was willing to sacrifice the very best He had to purchase our loyalty. It was extravagantly expensive for God. But because God saw our immense value and worth, and because He knew our built-in capacity for potential usefulness on the planet, He chose to pay the price.

He valued us, and He desired our friendship on a voluntary basis. He passed on making robot-humans; He wanted to make it possible for us to choose to reach out and touch Him voluntarily. God knew it would be costly to pay for the sins of the world, and He "so loved the world that He gave His only begotten Son, that whoever believes in [Jesus] should not perish but have everlasting life"—starting now. Our redemption is more than a heavenly fire insurance policy; it also is a PAID IN FULL policy for us to be restored to a relationship with God.

Christ did not die for beings without value.

◆

The death of Christ on the cross was not a waste. God endured watching Jesus suffer through all He did because it was necessary to purchase back—or redeem—His most prized creation: human beings.

Redeem Your Pawn Ticket

If you were to continue thinking of yourself as the chair analogy suggests, as an object camouflaged with false coatings, you could almost say that the real you is in Satan's Pawn Shop; you've been sold out. Someone (a *real* prince of a guy) has paid the price for your redemption, but you haven't yet cashed in on your rightful possession!

That process begins when you confess your need to be redeemed and you accept Jesus Christ as your Lord. It's quite simple, really. You give up your life in exchange for a new life from God. You hand over the controls to your sputtering, faltering life, and God places the life of Christ inside you. This life is the kindling wood that sparks a warm fire of God in your life, bringing to life the real person He wanted you to become.

Don't Keep the Prince Waiting!

Is it hard for you to believe that God really cherishes you, enjoys you, and delights in you—the real you? A disillusioned teenager, struggling with rejection and trying to believe that God loved her, reported a life-changing dream. She saw herself in a mirrored ballroom, with tuxedos and ball gowns floating around the dance floor. A handsome bearded man approached her; she turned her gaze to the floor. As he asked her to dance, he whispered, "I'm crazy about you!"

She was shocked as she looked up and recognized the man: He was Jesus!

That same Jesus wants to have this dance with you—for the rest of your life. If you haven't yet invited the Prince of Peace into your life, I encourage you to admit that you need Him—right now. Confess your sins and ask Him to enter your life, to be the transforming power you need.

I remember the night, as a teenager, I filled my God void with the Living Truth. As I sat listening, attending an event that I expected would turn out to be a Holy Roller meeting, I gave my full attention to the preacher, a young Southerner named Billy Graham. He spoke the truth—not just philosophically or off the top of his head but from the Bible.

Quoting from 1 John, he read, "He who has the Son has life; he who does not have the Son of God does not have life." I knew I had no sense of real life inside me, apparently because

I had never asked Jesus to enter my life. I'd been to church with my mother for years, and I had been operating on the mistaken idea that you get your religion from your family. That night I learned an important lesson.

God doesn't have any grandchildren.

◆

When Billy Graham gave his invitation to know Christ, I made my simple surrender, to receive the truth—that Jesus loved me. I decided to give up—to relinquish my life—and that's when I began to discover the real me. When we find Him, we find ourselves as well!

Let's erase our past assumptions and recognize the truth that God *does* love us—in spite of ourselves. Despite our failings and resistance, God still is sending out His love vibes toward us. God is not about to renege on that decision He made ages ago when He sent Jesus to pay for our sins. It's a done deal!

We can enjoy that truth and begin to build on this firm foundation of love, or we can reject it and try to fill the void in our lives with cheap substitutes. If we refuse the truth, we'll search around, trying to build a good feeling about ourselves on some other unsure footing besides His love. When the foundation of self-image is solidly on the Rock (Jesus Christ), we have a dependable footing on which to build a positive identity and a workable faith.

More Blessed to Give Than to Receive

Having received the truth of Christ, we are equally blessed in giving something back to Him. We offer our Creator all our fears and heartaches, along with the unanswered questions of the past.

I want to encourage you to reach deep into the dark crevasses of your soul and to dredge up your worst fears. By exposing them to the Light, and bringing them out into the open, you hand them over to God and let them go.

What do you need to say to God?

I'd never put it into words before, but one day I blurted out, "Okay, I'm afraid I'm gonna get cancer, like so many of the people in my family." In the very speaking of those words, which had long lurked in my subconscious mind, I felt a release, and I received insight as well.

That doesn't make much sense, Lee, the thought came to me. *Most of the heartache and disease in your natural family can be traced to alcoholism and chain-smoking. You don't live that lifestyle; don't sweat it!*

What a release!

What secret fear do you need to give to the Lord? Put words to it and get it out:

"I'm afraid my husband will leave me."

"I fear our country won't ever recover."

"I'm so worried about my child . . . could it be drugs?"

"How could I face another divorce?"

"I think we're headed for bankruptcy."

There is hope for us—even if we find ourselves confronting the worst-case scenarios threatened by our gnawing anxieties. Like mushrooms, our fears tend to grow in the dark. We must crack open ourselves to God and to one another, admitting these faults to one another and praying for one another so we can be healed (James 5).

Fear knocked at my door, faith answered, and there was no one there.
Evangelist Billy Sunday

Relatively Speaking

Being a genuine member of the family of God may well turn out to be a lot easier than being in your birth family! It happens quite simply:

> But as many as received Him, to them He gave the right to become children of God (John 1:12).

Receiving Christ causes us to be born into the family of God; our relationship is secure. The rest of relating to God is up to us; we qualify for fellowship with Him, and we are on our way to cultivating a friendship with Jesus. Relating to Christ involves getting real with God—no phoney baloney. Of course, He already knows everything about our thought lives, our fears, our needs, and our failures. But He wants to hear us speak the truth to Him. Tell Him where you are:

"I've fallen in love with X."
"I resent the shape of my body."
"I hate my kids right now."
"I confess You seem far away, Lord."
"I've made a huge financial mistake."
"I have no more strength—I'm empty."
"I'm doubting Your promises because I'm so disappointed in what's happened."

We need to understand that relating to Christ is actually relating to "the Spirit of truth" (John 14:17). The more truthful we get with God, with others, and with ourselves, the freer we'll feel inside. And the more we'll be able to count on Him to meet some of our deepest emotional needs.

Our need to feel accepted. Our unconscious baiting of others to tell us we are approved will be replaced by the awareness that we have already been "accepted in [Jesus] the Beloved."

Our need for approval. As we accept the fact that we are justified by faith before God, we will relax back on the grace of God. Now we can feel good about ourselves because of what Christ has done, not on the merit of our own performance. We've actually been "accounted for righteousness" (Rom. 4:5).

Our need to feel unashamed. We'll soon stop playing the blame game on ourselves—we always wind up losers in that game. Rather than count our failures, we can cultivate the new creature God has allowed us to be in Him. Take a look

at some of the wonderful attributes of that new creature—
the real you—in Christ. Read these truths out loud:

> I am saved forever by grace through faith.
> I am born again!
> I am accepted, forgiven, and loved by God.
> I am a servant of the Most High God.
> I am a new creature, dead to sin, alive to God.
> I am walking in newness of life.
> I am a temple for the Holy Spirit to dwell in.
> I am at peace with God.
> I am a partaker of the divine nature.
> I am a part of the earthly body of Christ.
> I am a citizen of the kingdom of God.
> I am a soldier of Christ and a fisher of men and women.
> I am a minister of reconciliation.
> I am a child of God, beloved by Him!

Sometimes you hear people say, "God loves you and
so do I." With the same confidence, you should also be able
to say, "God loves *me*, and so do I!"

Step No. 2: Remove the Layers

When you discover you are leading only half a life, the other half will haunt you until you live it!

The goal is to become a whole person, to enjoy a sense of completeness and satisfaction in the incomparable design God has for each of us as individual women. That's why it's necessary to examine any elements from the past that may have caused you to shut down a part of yourself. You need to experience wholeness in the sense of who God has made you to be—warts and all. Coming out of denial will enable you to rediscover that person God created you with the potential to become with your glorious uniqueness.

A sense of satisfaction and confidence in God's choices for us will lead us to admire Him, and will protect and defend His decision to make us the way we are. At the same time, a spiritual perception of wholeness can free us of pretense and cover-up, so we can relax into the real us. We must be diligent to unearth the original identity, despite the mixed messages that may come from our self-talk.

If you ever watched someone refinish a valuable piece of antique furniture, you can appreciate the stripping process. For emotional stripping and cleansing, we have been given a potent, indispensable product:

Forgiveness is a most powerful stripping agent.

◆

A generous application of forgiveness begins the dissolving process, which is necessary to reveal the real, priceless material underneath. Applying it to past hurtful experiences can bring to light your true natural beauty again. No more does the ugly coating of bitterness need to disguise the real you. You'll have to absolve the others who've painted you, as well as the circumstances that have caused you to camouflage yourself.

How do you start? You may find it helpful to start at the beginning—to be sure you're covering all the essentials in your stripping process. You may want to journalize or make a list of the people you feel have wronged you—splashed some other color on you or convinced you that who you are just isn't quite right. When you review your childhood memories, what stands out?

Have Paintbrush, Will Parent

Many Americans classify themselves as having been raised in a dysfunctional home, and that very home is probably where they first were told their feelings were wrong. For this reason, many adults have trouble sharing the truth about how they feel now; it was risky business when they were growing up. Where is that joyful child God meant each of us to be? Many parents have a prescribed way of behaving—etched in stone—and their children must subscribe to that way:

> "We don't do it that way; this is the way we do it in *our* family."
> "We are Catholics and always will be."
> "This is the way *we* celebrate Thanksgiving."
> "A lady always wears her gloves."
> "Don't make us look bad."

Unwittingly, parents often give their kids the message that whatever they naturally feel is *not* okay. This dreadful way of enforcing false responses can crush the spirit of an expressive child and convince him or her that the reaction is unacceptable. This is what he or she hears:

> "There's nothing to be afraid of."
> "You have no reason to cry."
> "Settle down; don't get so excited."
> "Don't think that way; that's stupid."
> "Don't be so curious."
> "You ask too many questions."
> "You talk too much."
> "Just forget about it and go on."

Of course, children who are expressing these emotions are not right or wrong—they are voicing genuine feelings. Today, your trouble with sharing the truth about how the real you feels may stem from your childhood when it was too risky to share.

> The past exists only in memory, consequences, effects.
> It has power over me only as I continue to give it my power.
> I can let go, release it, move freely.
> I am not my past; the future is not yet.
> I can fear it, flee it, face it, embrace it,
> and be free to live now.

Embracing the Past

Negative incidents in the past may disable us today if we continue to grant power to them. When we are convinced, by past experiences, that we are substandard or unworthy, we begin to abandon the true self. We forsake the authentic person and surrender to negative assumptions.

As I look back on some of my hard times, I am learning to thank God for the bad past experiences and to ask Him to reveal to me the way I should respond to them today. Rather than surrender to the idea that God is trying to wipe me out, I choose to see God the Father in a more positive light. I cling to the words of Jeremiah 29:11:

> I know the plans I have for you, says the LORD.
> They are plans for good and not for evil,
> to give you a future and a hope (TLB).

When we factor God's purpose and plan into our negative experiences, we can begin to cultivate a grateful spirit for the compassion and understanding these imperfections have developed in us. Life, whatever it has been up until now, has shaped us into the people we are today. I believe God is able to transform these negative experiences into good, and He can use them to maneuver us into the place He intended us to be.

The apostle Paul must have had his moments of doubt! In 2 Corinthians 11:25-29, he gives a partial listing of some of the undeserved, unfair treatment he received:

> Three times I was beaten with rods; once I was stoned; three times I was shipwrecked; a night and a day I have been in the deep; in journeys often, in perils of waters, in perils of robbers, in perils of my own countrymen, in perils of the Gentiles, in perils in the city, in perils in the wilderness, in perils in the sea, in perils among false brethren; in weariness and toil, in sleeplessness often, in hunger and thirst, in fastings often, in cold and nakedness—besides the other things, what comes upon me daily: my deep concern for all the churches. Who is weak, and I am not weak? Who is made to stumble, and I do not burn with indignation?

That dude had it rough! Yet he wasn't defeated by torturing himself with the question, Why did God let all these things come my way? Instead, he interpreted the events rightly, stating in Philippians 1:12: "The things which happened to me have actually turned out for the furtherance of the gospel."

The events of our lives, when we let God use them, become the mysterious and perfect preparation for the work He has called us to do.

◆

By the age of eighteen, I'd experienced my share of disappointments. Raised in a dysfunctional home with alcoholic parents, I was raped and became pregnant by a stranger. The baby girl I bore as a result was given up for adoption at birth. Then, twenty years later, my reunion with her became the subject of my book entitled *The Missing Piece.*

For a long time, the real Lee was buried under years of pretending and past hurts. In this mode it became easy for me to believe that my opinions, my personality, and my feelings were wrong, and thus the concealing process began. How important it is to release the hold the past has on us—to cut that umbilical cord to yesterday. Although we can't change history, we can change the effect the past has on the present. And a key element is forgiveness.

Forgive Those Who Have Trespassed Against You

Jesus couldn't have been more clear: if we do not forgive men and women their trespasses against us, our own trespasses will not be forgiven. We must apply the stripping agent of forgiveness and then begin to rip back, tear back, and peel back hostility, anger, and those heavy coats of disappointment and anxiety that keep us hidden.

Forgiveness is not an option; it is a commandment.

◆

Why continue to keep the real you hidden under layers of unforgiveness? It is an ugly, hard veneer. Others can't see you through it, although they quickly feel its toughness. Are you justified in your resentment? Maybe you are; that scoundrel really did a number on you. You could call a pity party, and many friends would come and bring a gift to cheer you up!

But here's the rub: those people you refuse to forgive are not suffering for it. They never think about it. But you do. Forgiveness is for revealing the true you; it is not for the sake of the offenders.

When you do not forgive, you permit your enemies to live rent free in your head. Evict them today!

◆

The Painted Victim

No doubt about it. Past offenses and unfair experiences can paint us into the victim corner where we contritely wear the badge of casualty. Unfortunately, that particular stance does not help us; it only enables us to remain in the same position, with no apparent way out.

I call this the victim syndrome. This particular veneer tends to mount up when we view the unfair events of our lives as having victimized us. Rotten, unfair, crummy circumstances continue to plague those who choose to remain in the victim syndrome.

Some people's entire identity is wrapped up in being a victim. But God did not create any of us as victims—let's not choose to stay that way. As author Barbara Johnson has reminded us,

Pain is inevitable; misery is optional!

◆

Grant God His Pardon

God doesn't do anything wrong. But many of us, coated over by painful past experiences, have subconsciously come to blame God for some of the things that have gone wrong. After all, He didn't intervene, did He? He could have prevented that hurtful experience, but He was silent.

A friend said to me, "Well, I feel my life is a performance for which I never got a chance to rehearse—and that's not fair!" She's right—we never got to see the script, and now we're forced to ad-lib as we go along. One of the lines we have to remember to use again and again is "I forgive you." Sometimes we find ourselves saying it to God, not because He has done wrong, but because we've blamed Him for our hurts.

I recall the time when my husband's protective shield of hardness was stripped off as he forgave God. His first two precious Christian wives had died tragic deaths, and God hadn't intervened to prevent the tragedies. A heavy burden was lifted off Hal's spirit as he let go of his resentment and disappointment and released the bitterness he'd held in his heart against his heavenly Father.

Do you feel God may have failed you? Did you think He had promised you something, and then He didn't provide it? Did He take someone precious out of your life? Did He allow you to fail when you counted on Him to help you succeed? Why not take a moment to pray and tell Him all about it? Confess the hostility, anger, anxiety, and fear you developed from that disillusionment. Let Him know that you know that He is God, that He bought you with a price, and that you know His ways are above your ways.

The real truth is that God's heart was also broken over that incident. But invariably, God will somehow be the fall guy. In California where I live, we often get shaken by earthquakes, and we may suffer some structural damage to our homes and property. But will the insurance companies cover this loss? No way. They will quickly claim they are not responsible because that disaster was an act of God. But it was not an act of Father God; it was simply an act of nature. When Jesus (representing God to us) was on the earth, He never caused the storms. He only commanded, "Peace, be still," to the chaos.

God does not always prevent evil from coming into our lives, but He is the only One who can make good out of evil!

◆

The I-Should Syndrome

Have you blown it? Royally? Join the group of real people who are in the same boat with you. If you have freely received forgiveness, why not also freely give it to yourself? Consider this Scripture from a woman's point of view:

> Happy is she who does not condemn herself in what she approves. But she who doubts is condemned . . . because she does not eat from faith (Rom. 14:22-23).

Refuse to spatter yourself anymore with the I-know-I-should-have's.

"I should have taken that job."
"I should have moved when I had the chance."
"I should have married Mr. X."
"I should have gone back to school."

Don't *should* on yourself anymore!

Recognizing the truth of God's love for us supplies us with the courage we need to begin stripping down to what He originally created. If He thought that original creation was so worthwhile, we'll be pleased with what we find underneath it all.

Valerie waited for me after I spoke. Her eyes were lowered, and it seemed difficult for her to speak; she felt she was bothering me. "I wanted to say thanks," she stammered. "You see, I always knew that I blew it—my three abortions, I mean. And now that I'm battling cervical cancer, I know I deserve that, too. But when you said we don't have to pay for our sins—that's why Jesus died—it dawned on me. God is not punishing me for my sins; I asked Jesus to forgive me years ago. Tonight I forgave myself, and I feel like thirty pounds have been lifted off my back. Thanks so much."

Jesus has already paid the price for your sins—your failures and bumbling mistakes. Whether you receive forgiveness and enjoy it or not is up to you. It might be a lot like three-year-old Michael who flushed his mom's good earrings down the toilet—along with some crayons. After his mother explained why it was wrong, Michael cried tears of repentance. Of course, Mom assured him that she had forgiven him, and that everything was okay.

But Mikey felt so bad about what he'd done that he wouldn't come out of his room; he felt like such a bad boy. Try as she might, Mom kept assuring her son of her love and forgiveness, but Mikey didn't buy it. She assured him that he was more important than a pair of earrings, and that she wanted him to forget the whole incident. Eventually he did.

Much like Mikey, too many of us have not yet received the forgiveness and love from God that Jesus paid for. Not only have we already been forgiven (believe it or not!), God considers us new creations—cleaned up and fit for His service. Scripture promises,

> Therefore, if anyone is in Christ, he is a new creation; old things have passed away; behold, all things have become new (2 Cor. 5:16).

The forgiveness we ask for is not a one-time thing. I find myself daily confessing wrong attitudes and unfair judgments, seeking cleansing. How wonderful to know that Christ's death on the cross provided forgiveness not only for the past—but for the future as well.

This stripping process of forgiveness will go on as long as you live—forgiving someone else or yourself, or coming to terms with God's sovereignty. Underneath it all you'll discover that you actually do have what it takes to become the person God equipped you to be. You'll be less aware of nagging fears, of intimidation, rejection, embarrassment, or shame. When you feel more sure of who you are, you can more effectively handle a challenging task, attempt something you never before would have dared to tackle, and be better equipped to handle criticism.

Once you are convinced that God did not shortchange you, you'll have the courage to seek and find the spiritual gifts He has invested in you. Identifying these supernatural giftings may have more to do with attributes, values, and natural tendencies than it does with a present course of action. For instance, if a woman defines herself by the label *mother,* her life will feel fruitless when she faces the empty nest. But if she sees her calling as *nurturer* rather than mother, she will carry her inner gifts beyond the empty bedrooms and lavish them on others around her who need her encouragement.

If you feel like royalty, being asked to clean toilets won't make you a slave. If you feel mentally competent, crawling on the floor to entertain toddlers won't diminish you. If you are an ambassador, carrying someone else's luggage won't make you a porter. Performing a humble task is no longer humiliating.

When you feel graced, no menial task of serving is disgraceful.

◆

The Do-Over Life

In the movie *City Slickers* starring comedian Billy Crystal, one of his buddies had miserably failed. He'd had an affair and lost his wife and kids and job. He was hanging his head in shame and discouragement. Billy's character compassionately said, "Hey, remember when we were kids and you'd throw the ball and it would land in a tree or out of bounds? We'd all yell in unison 'do over!' Phil, your life is a do-over!"

The same goes for you—think of your life as a do-over! It wasn't a total loss. You weren't doomed to fail. You've always got a chance to try again. And you're not alone. Many famous historical figures have used this do-over idea:

- Winston Churchill failed the sixth grade.
- Leo Tolstoy flunked out of college.
- Einstein was four years old before he could speak and seven before he could read.
- Louisa May Alcott was told by an editor that she "could never write anything that had popular appeal."
- Beethoven's music teacher once said of him, "As a composer, Ludwig is hopeless."

Many men and women in history have failed and gotten back up again. They may have been temporarily out, but they didn't listen to the referee counting! One of them was this well-known man—can you recognize him by his track record?

- Dropped out of grade school.
- Ran a country store.
- Went broke.
- Took fifteen years to pay off his bills.
- Had an unhappy marriage.
- Ran for Congress, lost twice.
- Ran for Senate, lost twice.
- Delivered a speech that became a classic; but the audience was indifferent.
- Was attacked daily by the press.
- Was despised by half the country.

Despite all this, imagine how many people all over the world have been inspired by this awkward, rumpled, brooding man who signed his name *Abraham Lincoln*.

I'm so glad Jesus came to give us a new life and a new start! He said He came for the sick, not for the well—for the people who will honestly admit they've blown it and need help. Those of us who fail, stumble, and fall are the very ones who need a healing word from the Great Physician. I believe He may be saying to us, "Your life is a do-over. Do it over with Me!" And that encouragement to get up and try again comes not only with a positive push, but Jesus promises to live inside all those who surrender to Him. His help on the inside promises real change on the outside.

You always pass failure on the way to success!

◆

Holy Failures?

The history of failures who became winners goes back farther than contemporary history. Scripture is filled with similar accounts. Because the Bible is so honest and so realistic in presenting its heroes, we can take heart. God knew there was a phase in their lives when their behavior and lifestyle hid the real person He had originally created. Just like them, we can choose to do right after doing wrong.

The *real* Eve was not a failure but God's prototype for a woman.
The *real* King David was not an adulterer but a man after God's own heart.

The *real* Rahab was not a harlot but a woman who risked her life for others.

The *real* Peter was not an impulsive braggart but a humble man who would powerfully preach the gospel.

The *real* Mary Magdalene was not a wicked woman but was entrusted with being the first witness to Jesus' resurrection.

The *real* Jesus was not a humble carpenter but the Christ; not just a messenger but the Message—our Messiah.

Beware: The Painters Are Ready!

Now that you've decided to strip away the many coatings of paint that hide the real you, let me give you a word of warning. People are standing in line, ready to tell you who you should be now that you've started the do-over process.

The more unsure you are of yourself, the more they will feel led to instruct you. They are waiting to give you direction:

"You should get a different job."

"You oughta teach a Sunday school class."

"You should cut your hair."

"Going back to school is a dumb idea."

"You are too quiet."

"You could make something out of yourself."

Once you've consulted the Master Architect about your original design, don't consult amateurs to help you with the refurbishing process.

We know it is healthy to feel good about ourselves, yet it ain't easy to find the way to do it. I believe Jesus is the open Door to a positive self-perspective. No one truly comes to God the Father except by Jesus, according to Christ's own words (John 14:6). Maybe none of us can wholeheartedly find the way to our unabridged versions except by the way of Jesus, either. As He paves the way to God the Father for us, so He will help us blaze the trail toward our own peaceful, still waters in our self-discovery quest.

Hold the Paint!

Today, after many years of discovery, I am experiencing the joy and freedom of being consistently me, without changing myself to satisfy outside influences. I want to present myself as the same person at all times—whether I'm with the company VP or with the housecleaning gal. I don't want to pull inside my turtlelike shell when I feel intimidated or change color to blend in with the intimidating attitude of someone else.

That is what happened to that little child's chair I found. It kept changing its identity, and after being painted so many different colors, it lost its value. Many of us women do the same thing. We carry an invisible paintbrush in our purses, ready at all times to alter who we are to fit the occasion. We'll slap on a dab of one color or another right in the middle of a conversation and poof! we look different. Let's make a commitment to throw away our hidden paintbrushes.

The Paintbrush

I keep my paintbrush with me, wherever I may go,
in case I need to cover up,
so the REAL ME doesn't show.

I'm so afraid to show you ME, afraid of what you'll do,
you might laugh, or say mean things;
I'm afraid I might LOSE you.
I'd like to remove all my paint coats,
to show you the real, true me,
but I want you to try and understand—
I need you to LIKE what you see.
So, if you'll be patient and close your eyes,
I'll strip off my coats real slow . . .
Please understand how much it can hurt,
to risk letting the REAL ME show.

Now my coats are all peeled off,
I feel naked, bare, and cold.
If you still love me with all that you see,
you're my friend, pure as gold.
But I need to save my paintbrush,
and hold it in my hand,
I want to keep it handy,
in case someone doesn't understand.
So please protect me, my dear friend,
and thanks for loving me true;
just let me keep my paintbrush—
until *I* love *me*, too!

Step No. 3: Review the Present

> Though no one can go back and make a new start, anyone can start from now, and make a brand new ending.
>
> ── *Carl Bard, Gloomies*

No, we can't literally go back and make a new start. But looking objectively at the past helps us avoid repeated mistakes and allows us to move forward with forgiveness. Forgiveness, in turn, peels off some of the veneers we've layered on ourselves because of past hurts. Once the forgiveness process is under way and continuing on a daily basis, it's time for us to take a look at the present.

- What factors are causing us to stifle who we are?
- What elements are encouraging us to become all that we can be?
- Who presently intimidates us?
- Who triggers our negative emotions?
- Who makes us angry? Uneasy?

It's important for us to review and pinpoint our negative impulses and to keep in mind the situations or persons who trigger them. In the past, those feelings caused us to cover up, to cower down under the weight of their threat. However, God sees beyond these behaviors and will join us in our efforts to remove our facades. God's attitude is reflected in the perspective of the great Italian sculptor of the classic *David* statue.

I saw David through the stone, and began chipping away at everything that was not David.
Michelangelo

Your Ever-Present Houseguest

In northern California there is a strange tourist attraction called the Winchester House. It was built by the heiress to the Winchester fortune. Somehow, she had come to believe that as long as she kept building, as long as she could hear the sounds of construction going on, she would continue to live.

Today an odd, rambling structure stands as a monument to her superstition. As tourists pour through the maze of rooms and hallways, they find doors that lead into walls, windows that were built to view nothing, and stairs that climb to a drop-off.

Dr. Bob Munger wrote a fine piece entitled "My House: Christ's Home" in which he creates the metaphor of Christ living inside individuals who invite Him in. But what does the Lord find when He moves in? Perhaps we've put on some additions like Mrs. Winchester did that are totally unnecessary: useless rooms, corridors without a destination. These are the things—the unreal things—that we can begin to eliminate from our lives.

In 1 Corinthians 3, Christ is referred to as the Master Builder; He is the original architect. You are in the process of cleaning out anything that was not in the original plan for you. Have you remodeled His original simple plan for you? Have you added on appealing, artificial facades with nothing underneath to support them? Let's take a look at some of the areas in which you need to do a little tearing down so that the rebuilding of your life can move forward smoothly.

The important thing about your lot in life is whether you use it for building or parking.

◆

Renovation No. 1: Your Ever-Present Emotions

A recovering alcoholic friend of mine said to me, "As an insecure teenager, I quickly discovered that I could really be myself when I drowned myself in booze. Suddenly my shy personality disappeared, and I was the life of the party. It felt great!"

Did you know that there's a healthy form of intoxication? The new wine of God's Holy Spirit has a far better effect on people than the alcohol my friend described! The Spirit wants to set our spirits free so we are able to behave in an unintimidated, childlike manner. The apostle Peter once had to correct a crowd that misinterpreted the uninhibited, joyful behavior of the disciples. He said, "These are not drunk, as you suppose" (Acts 2:15).

Feelings that bridle and constrain us ought to be put aside, but we have to choose whether we can get rid of them legally or illegally. Some of the addictive ways men and women use to overcome inhibitions include these:

Prescription drugs
Alcohol
Recreational drugs (illegal)
Hobbies
Religious activities
Shopping

The list is endless.

Why do we build up inhibitions in the first place? In our modern civilization, we're seldom encouraged to take the time to process our emotions. We are on the fast track, and when something hurts, we quickly change the subject. Are we so absorbed in our activities that we deny ourselves time for self-evaluation and healing?

Next time you feel wronged or hurt, make a decision to identify your feelings. What are they telling you about yourself? When you deny your emotions the fresh air of expression, you suffocate them, and your real self begins to wither.

Are my feelings right or wrong? You may be honestly seeking righteousness when you ask, but it's the wrong question. Emotional responses are totally involuntary. Emotions themselves are not right or wrong—they just *are*. And they are a natural part of being human. How you deal with them and what kind of behavior they produce determine whether you are right or wrong.

Risky Business

It's risky business, this matter of emotional honesty. It's scary to purposefully allow others to know who we are. If we open ourselves up to others and gamble vulnerability, we become unprotected. We may be subject to ridicule, and we could be thought of as petty or foolish.

Perhaps you've taken a chance in the past and expressed your opinion or ventured out with your feelings, only to be slapped down. Therefore, you convinced yourself that your impressions were wrong. It is now easier for you to withdraw rather than reveal yourself and take the chance of being wounded again. Who wants to volunteer for any more pain? But without risking the chance of injury, you won't ever enjoy the validation of your friends or discover your real self.

Let me give you a personal example. For years I used to dread Christmas because I felt so intimidated by my many "domesticated" friends whom I knew would bring me lovely baskets filled with homemade goodies. I guess I felt I didn't qualify; women are expected to give delicious fresh-baked gifts at Christmas. I am, indeed, a woman; however, I must admit that my only domestic quality is that I live in a house. Help! I'm domestically impaired!

But in recent years, I've learned to look forward each Christmas to giving my own unique gift, something that more accurately reflects the real me. Each Christmastime I distribute a special booklet, "Jokes for the John." My friends share it with their holiday guests, who also enjoy it. It's amazing to me how much folks appreciate this strange gift—even more than gingerbread cookies! And now I'm afraid I've built a reputation for myself; by November, friends have started asking me, "When is our joke book coming?"

In his book *Why Am I Afraid to Tell You Who I Am?* author John Powell expresses sentiments you may recognize. He says, "If I tell you who I am, you may not like who I am—and that's all I have!" He's right. It is a risk. But we must take the risk of feeling awkward or unworthy in order to express our individuality and become authentic.

Renovation No. 2: Your Roles

Are you the real you at work? If people from your household happened to walk into your office, would they recognize you? Do you act the same whether at a board meeting or at a church gathering? The goal is to authentically demonstrate your real self—to be exactly the same person in any role you adopt.

Be honest with yourself. Does your life feel like a TV series? Maybe you feel more like you are acting out a part; you're in the proper costume and the right makeup, you know your lines, and you act like you are expected to when you are on the set. But why not surprise them all? Why be so predictable? Begin right where you are.

One day I was broadcasting a radio interview when a caller bravely blurted out to me, "You know, I'd love to be the real me, but I can't move to Phoenix!"

"Why do you have to move to Phoenix to be the real you?" I asked.

"Because I'm an artist at heart, and there is a colony of dedicated artists in Phoenix. I know I could truly express myself there."

"But if the real you is truly an artist, why does she have to be a Phoenix resident? Why not practice right now—where you live? Sign up for a couple of art classes. Explore your gift now. Why do you have to move?"

Don't move unless you are moving closer to your originality. Fulfill the will of God for your life.

◆

Child Rearing—Encouraging Your Real Child

Parental ideas about roles are often imposed on children. In fact, childhood may have been the very time we first began to "act." Many adults recall being overcorrected, blamed, and shamed.

Whether you are a foster parent, an adoptive parent, a stepparent, or a birth parent, it probably didn't take long for you to discover that you were not the only one who determined the personality of your children. A night-person kid can be birthed by two day-person parents. Even if you have four children, each one can be totally different and much unlike either parent. Our job is to encourage our offspring to discover and appreciate their uniqueness. We can teach them that being different is not wrong.

Train up your child in the way he or she SHOULD go . . . not in the way the parent has predetermined the child should go, if you were to say things like, "You'll be a doctor like your father" or "Don't let the family down by wasting your life as a musician." Cookie-cutter parenting is not God's way.

Not in the way the child COULD go . . . if we manipulate him and pattern him after the image we have in mind.

Not in the way the child WOULD go . . . if she were left alone to battle peer pressure, or if we abandon her and leave her without parental guidance.

But to assist and encourage the child . . . in discovering what God has naturally patterned him or her for. Help kids explore what "feels natural" to them, and encourage them to explore their innate desires and dreams.

Self-Improvement School?

Parents aren't the only ones who have an idea about what role you'd like to play and where you'd like to play it. There will always be well-meaning friends who think they know what's best for you. And these Job's friends, as I call them, are always biting at your heels with helpful advice and constructive criticism. The more spiritual among them will cloak their judgments in spiritual terms:

"I feel led to share this with you . . ."
"The Lord showed me that you ought to . . ."

"I've been praying for you, and I think the Lord has given me a word for you . . ."

"You know, I really love you in the Lord, but there's something I have to tell you . . ."

"Can't you see that God's trying to teach you an important lesson?"

When confronted with criticism, we tend to forsake what is natural for us and to obediently bow to the whims and wishes of those who intimidate us.

Chuck Swindoll describes this process so well as he tells of a very prestigious School for Self-Improvement—for animals.

When the duck checked in, he was clearly a great swimmer. But he was advised that in order to become a well-balanced person, he should learn how to climb. And his struggle began.

Meanwhile the squirrel arrived at the admissions office and was told that his task was to ignore the ease with which he could climb; his challenge was to learn to swim. This caused great frustration for the squirrel—and his teacher.

And when the majestic eagle signed in, his talent for flying wasn't interesting to the powers-that-be. Mr. Eagle was ordered to abandon his natural instinct to fly and instead was instructed to learn how to run. If he truly wanted to become a more well-rounded, stable individual, he would submit to the required discipline.

I see so many eagle-women straining to lay eggs—someone has convinced them they are chickens! Don't you know some folks who are naturals for one job, while they are stressing out in another? We allow people to pigeonhole us, to back us into a corner with their manipulation. All the while God, our chief instructor, is trying to get the message across to us. He would call from the heavens, "But, My child, you find it difficult because I never gifted you for that. I never asked you to do that. It is hard for you to go against what I wired you for."

How many of us are guilty of the desires of our hearts, and we're trying to make ourselves something that we are not. No wonder it feels so unnatural!

To discover me is to discover my mission!

◆

Fatigue and stress often occur when we do things we were never meant to do, projects we were not gifted to do. Why do we make it so tough on ourselves?

In the movie *Chariots of Fire*, the character Eric Liddell says to his sister, "God made me to run, and when I run I feel His pleasure!" When you do the things God wants you to do—when you are in the process of becoming the person He has wanted you to be—you'll discover all the gifting you need is present! And, like Eric, you'll sense God's pleasure with you. Furthermore, you'll soon recognize that others are noticing the "natural" change in you. They'll like it. It will feel right.

Are you a natural for the role you're playing?

Does the work you are doing feel instinctively right?

Renovation No. 3: Your Fears

"The fear of man brings a snare," warns Proverbs 29:25, and many of us have become ensnared in a false identity we've developed because of this fear. We're forever asking ourselves, What will people think? Perhaps if we'll learn to fear the right person—God—we'll begin to be ourselves.

I am learning more and more about the real Lee as I make a conscious choice to face my fears, head-on, and take the plunge to confront them. Usually, fears loom larger in the imagination than they do in reality.

For instance, I generally tend to feel intimidated when confronted by someone in authority. In the all-wise doctor's office, I clam up. When stopped by a traffic cop, I humbly and meekly ask, "Where do I sign?" Sitting on the set with a talk show host, I hold back, fearing his or her interrogation, all too aware of my inadequacies. Even facing an assertive saleswoman, I tend to beg her for mercy, trying to return my damaged item as if I were the one who had damaged it.

What are your natural fears? They can pile up and leave you scared of your own shadow if left unconfronted. Do you fear speaking in public? That's not unusual: fear of public speaking is the number one fear of all Americans. By the way, the second most common fear is fear of death. I suppose that means that at a funeral, most Americans would rather be the person in the casket than the survivor giving the eulogy.

Are you fearful about something? Overcoming fear is sometimes as basic as doing the thing you fear. Consider the following possibilities:

Do you fear speaking up in church? *Risk it next time.*

Frightened about going back to school? *Sign up for just one course.*

Fear what would happen if "they" know your secret? *Expose the truth.*

Dread confronting your friend? *Start testing her (or him) for openness.*

Anxious about facing a relative? *Bite the bullet and call or write a note.*

I think there's quite a difference between an aggressive woman and an assertive one. I visualize an aggressive woman as a pushy broad elbowing her way rudely through life, demanding her rights. Meanwhile, an assertive woman leaves a more pleasant impression as a healthy individual who is stepping forward to claim her rights and to seek justice. By not fearing other people and by being assertive, you can take the risks necessary to become the real you.

If you're not doing something that scares you, you're not living up to your potential.

◆

Renovation No. 4: Your Relationships

If we are honest, we'll admit that we all enjoy the heartwarming feeling of being liked, accepted, and approved. It's imperative for you—and me—to be sure that the person being validated in your body is the real you; whatever you do, don't alter yourself to get that approval. If we transform ourselves to get strokes, we become creatures not unlike puppies—panting and wagging our tails, looking pitifully into the eyes of someone we're begging to pat us on the head.

Do you have friends or family members who cause you to feel intimidated or second class? Why not refuse to give them your permission to intimidate you the next time? The good news is this: we have control over our feelings, and when we make the right choices, the situation can change. In reality, no one else can cause us to feel the way we do, whether angry, rejected, or hurt. All our feelings are triggered inside us, according to the habit patterns we've established.

For instance, I remember being in the middle of a speech when I noticed three gals entering the back of the room, obviously late for the meeting. I was fascinated to observe their totally different reactions to the feeling of being late.

One woman nervously looked around, hating the embarrassing feeling of having to go to the front row for a seat.

Another gal was obviously ticked; she was sure the meeting had been announced for a later time—she was actually early!

The third woman stood in the threshold with a grin on her face; she was so tickled that she missed only about fifteen minutes!

Obviously, no one in that room made them feel that way! They all reacted in accordance with their habit patterns of behavior.

Do You Have a Fever?

I used to think that my moods and attitudes would be set for the day by others. I spent years acting like a thermometer, going around each morning taking the temperature of all my household, shyly asking, "How are you today? Are we going to have a nice day?" I set my mood according to everyone else's.

Now I am much more like a thermostat. I wake up in the morning and say, "Lord, I'm setting my temperature on fair and mild today! I won't let these people get me down!"

Real You Friendships

From now on you can commit yourself to real you friendships and little by little become more and more the original you with the people around you. After all, if others love only the front you've put up, they are not worthy of your friendship. Every human being needs a few genuine friends who encourage the real you to break out!

Ask yourself a few basic questions about any friendships in question:

- Would I still try to develop a friendship if I just met the person today?
- Does the relationship enhance me?
- Does the relationship diminish me?
- What do I receive from this relationship?
- Do I feel God is happy with the relationship?
- Am I being honest with myself—or deceiving myself—about the friendship?

- ◆ What keeps me from ending the relationship: fear? loyalty? habit? coercion?
- ◆ If waning, is the association worth rejuvenating?

Being vulnerable with the right people can bring the deepest sense of joy and affirmation. There is such satisfaction in consciously placing yourself at risk, only to have a friend say, "Wow! I can't believe you said that. I've felt that way for years, but I never had the courage to admit it." A genuine emotional connection happens when you choose to become accessible and expose the real you.

Emotional Tightwads Are Uptight!

Take a few moments to review your current friendships. List these folks in three categories. It can be so liberating to admit in which category a friendship falls.

It's easy to spot the givers; they add to your life. They are the *plus* people (+). Being with them is an encouragement; it is refreshing. They put up with your moods and struggle through your difficulties, encouraging you all the way. They are in your balcony. And they're not afraid to speak the truth in love to you. These folks honestly value the real you, and they support you in expressing your true feelings.

You can also easily spot the takers; they subtract from your life. They are the minus people (–). They are definitely not givers—being with them drains you. They would just as soon the real you didn't show up or express an opinion. The takers tend to be codependent. And you may cooperate with them—enabling them to stay dependent on you for happiness. They are with the continuously needy, becoming their rescue ranger. Is ministering to these takers just another way of saying, "Please love me; can't you see that I'm helping you?"

And finally you'll classify some friends as neutral in your life—they neither give nor take; they're just there.

Take a moment now to jot down the names of your friends and associates under the category they most reflect. What a healthy evaluation!

Evaluating My Relationships

Givers:	Takers:	Neutral:
(+)	(−)	(0)
_____	_____	_____
_____	_____	_____
_____	_____	_____

When my husband and I sorted through our friendships, we were amazed to see how few honestly fell in the givers column. Most folks we spent time with were draining us dry; they were takers. Of course, to be a person who honestly cares about others, you need to be in a giving relationship with a few takers. But some of us are overrun with takers, and then we wonder why we are burned out. When Hal and I began to adjust our time spent in consideration of the chart, we made a healthy change.

How to Drop a Relationship

If you find, as we did, that you have too many takers on your list of relationships, and you face the fact that they are draining you faster than you can get refilled, it's time to divest yourself of the depleting associations.

You can try not being available whenever the person calls or drops by, but if this evasive method has no effect, you'll have to go for broke. Face off this person, or write if you must. But the substance of what you'll need to say is something like this:

"I appreciate our friendship, and in the past, I feel we've been good for each other. But frankly, lately I feel our relationship has become so one-sided that I am drained when we are together. From my perspective, it seems to be all taking and no giving on your part. I realize this is where you are right now, but let me tell you where I am right now.

"I find myself needing to take a breather. I have made the mistake of taking your problems on myself personally, and now I find that this is affecting my relationship with my family.

"I'd like to call a sabbatical in our friendship for a month's time. During this month I pledge myself to pray for you, but I want to avoid contact. When the month is over, let's get in touch again and reevaluate what comes next, okay? Remember this is not about you. It's about me. I need a break and a chance to pull back. Will you be a true friend and understand?"

Bringing a negative relationship to an abrupt end is preferable to dragging out the agony. As the old proverb says,

Which way is easier to cut off a dog's tail? All at once? Or just an inch at a time?

◆

Change What You Can!

The wisdom of the "Serenity Prayer" encourages us to action:

> God grant me the serenity to accept the things I cannot change, the courage to change the things I can, and the wisdom to know the difference.

If you are displeased with things about yourself, you can change some of them. As for other things—your height and nationality, for instance—you'll just have to learn to live with them. But if you know you need to lose weight, stop smoking, get out of debt, or change jobs, don't just talk about it, do it! And if it's an attitude change, start working on it—today.

A lively, friendly cafe manager greeted my husband, Hal, and me. He was a lighthearted fellow with a crisp British accent, always offering a smile and a joke as he seated his customers. Even though he worked in a high-stress job, he seemed to enjoy it. I couldn't resist asking him how he maintained his good spirits.

"It's something new for me," he replied. "I wasted too many years being shy and withdrawn. I wish I could redo the years in school and college, hiding behind my books, hoping nobody would notice me. As you can see, I'm quite short. I was teased unmercifully by my classmates all through school, and I decided to retreat. Then I was thrown into this public-contact restaurant business. I had to act friendly and outgoing.

"So I decided to turn it around and enjoy the ribbing, not resent it. Nowadays, I just join in the fun rather than let it devastate me." He continued with a gleam in his eye, "And my short stature doesn't bother me anymore; I make jokes about it. Now I actually think my short height is a plus, not a minus. It's an opportunity to give folks a chance to laugh at themselves—and *with* me, not *at* me."

What about you and your job? When you go to work, decide to get real. You don't have to laugh at the same old stories. You don't have to fall into the same rut. No more feeling intimidated, no more feeling put down, no more pretending to agree when you really don't.

Here's a key question for yourself:

Do I have to give up me to be loved by you?

Ask your friends, your family, your coworkers, and your church mates. If they don't love the real you, they are not worthy of your friendship. "Lay down your life for your friends," Jesus said. "Greater love has no man than this, that you lay down your life [openly reveal it!] for your friends."

I have spoken on this subject for years, and reports have begun to filter back to me that some women have felt I've granted them permission to honestly be themselves. After sessions, confessions began to flow:

- "I'm not the spiritual giant you think I am."
- "I've been hiding the fact that I smoke; I want to quit."
- "My family may look heavenly on Sunday, but when we hit the car it's a different story."
- "I am struggling with lustful thoughts."
- "I'm confused about what good it really does to pray; nothing seems to change."

These honest expressions come from the depths of *reality*, and they can lead only to more healthy relationships. They are solvents for dissolving the layers of falsehood that have separated us from others. Are you ready to get real? Here's your Certificate of Authorization:

Permission Granted

Permission is hereby granted to _____ to be HERSELF.
[your name]

I permit myself to risk expressing my genuine feelings and opinions; to communicate the real me in all its originality, without appearing to fit in or blend with the crowd. I permit myself to become the person God intended me to be, without fear, without apology, without wearing masks or other dishonest disguises.

_____
(signature)

_____
(date)

Step No. 4: Risk Revealing the Real You

When I think of the hundreds of things I might be, I get down on my knees and thank God I'm me.

Elsie Janis

I have learned that risk taking—in being authentic—is both challenging and rewarding. On one memorable occasion, I was sitting in my daughter's classroom while the teacher for the mentally gifted students (MGM) waxed eloquent during parents' night at the high school. I was straining to follow what was being said. I'm not your quickest learner anyway, and the teacher's rhetoric was completely over my head.

As I gazed around the room at the other parents, I had the feeling I wasn't the only one feeling intimidated by the instructor who was so diligently working to impress us. (It seemed to me he was educated beyond his capacity to comprehend.) In any case, I finally mustered up the courage to raise my hand.

"Yes?" inquired the patronizing instructor.

I took a deep breath and plunged in. "It seems to me that you are making an assumption here; an MGM

134

student doesn't necessarily come from an MGM parent. I'm not following you."

A rumble of snickers, sighs, and laughs around me broke into a chorus of "Yeah, that's right!" and "Me, too!" Taken off guard by the honesty of his audience, the instructor seemed disarmed. He smiled and relaxed. Once he came down to our level, he was able to communicate with us, and finally, we all got the picture.

Freedom comes from knowing and liking who you are, and it enables you to risk expressing yourself. And in doing so, you'll soon find out that we're all quite alike. We all desire acceptance and seek confirmation that we are okay. If we are getting affirmations from within ourselves—our *real* selves—we won't be straining to get them from others.

Lydia: Living on the Edge

Have you ever thought about the New Testament character Lydia? She was a fearless, successful woman, daring to be in business for herself in spite of first-century chauvinism. I wonder how many of her neighbors who were "proper" women gave her the cold shoulder. She apparently didn't know her place. In those days, it was unacceptable for a woman to run her own business. That was men's work. But Lydia knew who she was; she was a strong woman, and she realized it was not wrong to unashamedly reveal who she was.

Although she was not a Jew, she apparently had the chutzpah to sneak into a Jewish meeting to hear the apostle Paul speak about the Messiah, Jesus Christ. As she opened her heart to the truth, she bravely walked toward the shoreline with the Jews who wanted to be baptized. Influential woman that she was, she brought her whole household into the Christian faith.

Afterward, she courageously spoke up and invited Paul and his three companions (probably Silas, Luke, and Timothy) to stay at her house—despite the rumors that might fly through Philippi. "Why, the nerve of this woman! Inviting totally strange men, three guys she just met that morning, to stay under her roof! Who does she think she is?"

Lydia knew who she was; she did not shrink behind some sense of propriety. And once she met Jesus, she also knew that God was making her even stronger—and that was not wrong.

After Paul and Silas were thrown into prison, and God sent an earthquake to get them out, where did the men go to retreat? To Timothy's house? No. To James's or to John's? No. They headed straight for Lydia's house, confident she'd have the courage to take them in. Her strength of character and her fortitude to demonstrate the courage of her convictions became the foundation on which the New Testament church at Philippi would be built. I'm so glad the real Lydia dared rejection and didn't wimp out!

Dealing with Rejection

> May those who love us love us,
> And those who don't love us,
> May God turn their hearts.
> And if He doesn't turn their hearts,
> May He turn their ankles,
> So we will know them by their limping.

I love Christ's advice to His disciples, recorded in Matthew 10. He gave sound counsel about what to do if people don't receive you. Jesus didn't say, "Change to please them. Try to fit in. Don't offend. Conform to their image."

No, instead, He counseled His followers—then and now—that when others don't receive the real authentic message, "Depart from that house or city, shake off the dust from your feet." It's just as simple as that: we are supposed to speak the truth in love, and let the chips fall where they may!

Imprisoned in Self-Defense

Hal and I sadly watched Pastor Bill try to follow the success of the former pastor, who had a moral failure and was asked to leave. Even though the former pastor had little private integrity, he had great public presence and charisma, and he had endeared himself to his large congregation.

Pastor Bill had been struggling for two years to fill his predecessor's big shoes, to become the replacement the church was seeking. He was endeavoring to fit in and not rock the boat.

Then one rainy night everything changed.

Bill and his wife were flying in a buddy's light plane. The storm forced a crash landing that resulted in life-threatening injuries to Bill and a violently shaken-up wife. Their whole world was turned upside down and spilled out on the runway that night. Miraculously, Bill not only survived but struggled through physical therapy to totally restore all his faculties.

After a prolonged absence, one Sunday he returned to the pulpit for the first time.

Little did the congregation realize that through all of this, Pastor Bill was reclaiming the *real* Bill, and he was about to pour himself out to his congregation. His first Sunday back, he delivered a profound message. He was clearly in a physically weakened state, but his spirit shone through strong and true.

Speaking out of one of Paul's epistles written from jail, Bill confessed that over the past weeks he had discovered the jail he had built for himself. He'd finally recognized the imprisoning self-talk that had hindered him from being himself all those years.

> I have long lived in the shadow of another pastor—one whose track record I had to be measured by. I felt so inadequate to fit the bill. So I created a character and played it out here on the platform in front of you. I felt I was only as good as my last pulpit performance, on which I was scored each week.

He confessed the web he had spun for himself of negative expectations and insecurity, which caused him to expect disapproval and criticism. And he feared it would become a self-fulfilling prophecy.

But during his recovery, the outpouring of affection and prayer from the congregation changed Bill as a pastor. Under a canopy of love, he felt the freedom to express himself at last. He committed himself never to play the role of another pastor; he would more genuinely be the man he truly was—the man God had called to be their pastor.

You can guess the rest. The honest confession of his secret insecurities generated a true season of refreshing in his church and reunited it to become a strong body of believers, led by a pastor who was *real*—one who truly did break out of self-imposed jail!

Uniqueness cannot be satisfied if we submerge our creativity and subject our spontaneity.

◆

Are you ready to plan a breakout from your imprisoning, self-submerging thoughts? Have you been subjected to incarceration long enough to want to set that real person free? Christ came to proclaim liberty to the captives!

Living Inside Out

Like Pastor Bill, I'm endeavoring to live inside out. I'm trying to unveil my inadequacies and lay down my life. I think that when we begin confessing to one another—not our successes and our strengths, but our faults—we can pray for one another for healing. Speaking of our strengths separates us from one another; speaking of our weaknesses unites us.

When sportscaster Joe Garagiola gave a commencement speech at Saint Louis University, he had this advice for the graduates:

> All of us begin the race from the same starting line. . . .
> But I really believe the Lord gives each one of us two
> gift certificates when we're born. One is for a dream—
> my dream was to be a major league baseball player.
>   The other gift certificate lets you "take a chance." If
> the front door is locked, try the back door. If that's
> locked, too, try the window. Just don't be afraid to try,
> and don't be afraid to fail. Take a chance!

Life is more than a game of Monopoly, but why not pick up a chance card and go for it? Do not pass go—that's where you start. And don't collect just $200. Go for your full potential—go for the gold—the real you.

Telling It Like It Is

Because I am normally an up person, anyone who calls my home expects to hear some humorous recording on the answering machine or a cheerful voice on the other end of the phone. But take it from one who knows—a person who is constantly up is either out of touch with reality or on drugs!

One day a friend called to get cheered up. She said, "Hi, I'm down today. What's new with you?"

"I feel lousy," I responded.

There was a pause. "Whoa, that doesn't sound like you, Lee."

"Well, it *is* Lee today. I am struggling with a long list of *whys*. Elmer, a dear missionary friend of ours, is in a coma after suffering a stroke last week. I was counting on God performing a miracle for him, but it hasn't come yet. Honestly, I'm confused and a bit ticked about it, too."

My friend's tone quickly changed, "I'm sorry, Lee. That's a bummer. Can I pray for you?"

"Yes, please; I'm looking for the goodness of God today."

I found His goodness in that moment, through a genuine expression of love and concern in my friend's voice. But had I given her a business-as-usual response, she could have wound up draining out of me whatever little glimmer of life remained, recounting her problems. Instead, we both felt better.

Clear as Crystal

As we seek to reveal the real us, we are working on being see-through people—totally up front at all times. Of course, there are some times when we want to be private, and that's perfectly understandable. We don't want to always be living in a transparent glass house. But it's easy to get confused. I got so tickled when I heard this humorous story about California's Crystal Cathedral.

I heard an intriguing story about an older English-woman from a rural area of England who wasn't used to big cities. She was trying to plan a trip to see Anaheim's Disneyland, and she wrote to the Orange County Chamber of Commerce to inquire for a list of bed-and-breakfasts nearby.

The woman wanted to be sure the recommended rooms included a bathroom, but being a proper Britisher, she used the expression *W.C.* (*water closet*) and wrote: "Please inform me as to which of these rooms are close to the W.C.; this is vitally important to me."

The county employee, glancing at the letter, couldn't imagine what the W.C. referred to, unless the woman was writing about another tourist attraction near Disneyland known as the Crystal Cathedral. The county worker knew the church was totally made of glass, and thought the writer might be inquiring about (as some referred to it) the Window Cathedral—or W.C.

The request was forwarded to the cathedral, where it was referred to someone who assists in answering routine mail. Rather than correcting the Englishwoman, the writer replied in kind, referring to the cathedral as the W.C. She mailed off the following response:

Dear Madam:

> The Chamber of Commerce passed on your inquiry to me, and we are glad you have chosen to visit Orange County's tourist sites.
> It is my pleasure to inform you that the W.C. is situated very near to the rooms you are considering renting.
> You'll find it right in the middle of a beautifully land-scaped campus.
> My husband and I are regular attenders, and it may be of interest to you to know that two of our daughters were married in the W.C.!
> The W.C. is quite large, with a seating capacity for hundreds of people, surrounded on all sides by glass—and is open seven days a week, with regular guided tours.
> If you are in the habit of attending regularly, we would suggest you go with other women on Tuesday mornings at 9:15 for a very satisfying experience! As there are large crowds on Sundays, I suggest you come early, although there is usually standing room.
> Occasionally there can be a rush for seats (sometimes

more than 2 for each seat), but special seats are reserved
for the handicapped.
We have noticed many people bring their lunch and
make a day of it! I would especially recommend your
ladyship to go on Thursdays when there is a beautiful
organ accompaniment. The acoustics are excellent, and
even the most delicate sounds can be heard everywhere.
Please inform me when you will be coming, and I shall
be delighted to reserve an excellent seat for you from
which you can clearly see Dr. Robert Schuller, and even
be viewed by our television audience!
Hope you will visit soon.

Sincerely,
Betty, for the Cathedral

Let the Boundaries Be Visible

As the saying goes, "People in glass houses (or cathe-
drals) shouldn't throw stones." But all of us have boundaries
within which we operate for our own peace of mind. Each
of us secretly draws lines around our relationships. The
trouble is, because we are not always honest about those
lines, no one knows when he or she has violated the
boundaries. No alarm goes off. Most offended people don't
blow up or even let the hurt be known. It's easier to silently
retreat and perhaps never to see the troublesome person
again. When this is our habit, we leave a trail of broken
relationships behind us.

Instead of hiding your real feelings, practice making
the following statements:

- "I'm not comfortable with doing that; it bothers me."

- ◆ "I feel uneasy when we're gossiping."
- ◆ "I sense we're playing a game, and I want to be real."
- ◆ "It hurts me when you talk that way; I'm afraid."
- ◆ "I consider this verbal abuse, and I won't put up with it."
- ◆ "I've been coveting your wardrobe, and I admit I'm trying to imitate you. I'm just trying to discover the real me, I guess."
- ◆ "I need more challenge on my job; I'm getting bored."
- ◆ "I've seen you, and I'd like to get to know you better."
- ◆ "I sense there is a problem between us. Can we talk about it?"
- ◆ "I feel cramped, going nowhere. I need a change!"

Change Is Threatening

Whenever you take a chance by expressing yourself, you're running a risk. You may find support, or you may hit a wall of resistance. And as you change, your friends may not be aware of those changes right away. When your significant others see your physical body walk into a room, they'll expect the same person to be inside it. And when you respond differently from what they expect, they will be taken aback. They may even feel threatened. They aren't used to your being unpredictable.

When you do what you need to do to feel authentic, you'll soon discover just who loves you for who you are! Seek peace? Yes. But at *any* cost? No! That is too great a sacrifice.

Janet and Brian had been married almost ten years when she attended some classes I was giving on discovering

God's wonderful gift of the real you. Somehow Janet felt she had been given permission to be the way she naturally was, and she felt encouraged to pursue that person and explore her possibilities.

Soon she found herself trying out the new Janet on her husband.

"No," she responded one Friday night, "sorry, but I can't see that movie with you. But go ahead, enjoy it yourself."

"What's the matter with you?" he growled.

"Nothing, really. It's just that I've finally realized that the language and violence in those kinds of movies tend to stay with me. I can't get all of it out of my head. You walk out and forget it all, but I'm awake all night. I've decided I can't volunteer for that anymore. But go and have a good time."

"It never bothered you before. What's happening?"

"Well, I was never honest before. I want to be more open in our relationship about what hurts and what helps. I'm sure you'll understand."

Brian wasn't sure he understood at first. What in the world got into his amiable, never-makes-waves wife? But back at home, Janet felt a new sense of herself. She had risked honesty and the consequence of being put down for it. She also felt an inner peace from the Holy Spirit; He was glad she was recognizing the biblical admonition to "guard your heart."

As weeks went by, Brian gained a new respect for Janet, and they started discussing their plans together instead of doing whatever came into his head. Little by little, Janet's new perspective strengthened their marriage rather than weakened it.

Communicate the Change

The real you is not a chameleon, magically transforming into the image of anyone she is with. Don't continue to change your opinion to resist making waves. Why hide your convictions in order to fit in? You must not submerge your feelings to oblige or change your priorities to appease.

Practice communicating your genuine feelings in every possible arena.

To your boss: *I think I've given you the wrong impression, and I want to straighten it out. I do have a life outside this office, but I've been reluctant to say no to the demands of this job. I need to communicate this to you and make some changes in my workload.*

To your spouse: *I haven't been honest with you. I have some needs that are not being met. We're always so busy that I've not taken the time to tell you where I'm at. How about tonight?*

To your child: *I'm feeling kind of shut out lately. I really want a closer relationship with you. What can we do to get started?*

To your parents: *I need to let you know in advance that I don't think we can come out again this Christmas. I've been afraid of hurting you, so I haven't challenged our annual tradition, but I feel the need for my own family to be alone this Christmas.*

To your friend: *It seems to me our friendship has deteriorated. Somehow we only share negatives with each other, and we aren't doing each other any good! Let's talk about it, okay?*

Each time you practice expressing your honest, open feelings it will get a little easier. Over a period of time, you'll begin to feel so proud of yourself, and you'll be more aware of God's empowerment. He has implanted in your character the strength it takes to be yourself.

Practice Makes Potential Possible

Let's face it. Our all-too-prominent egos get us into so many things we should have said no to. Once the unreal you senses the pressure to conform, it will eke out an "Okay, I don't mind" or "Whatever—I'll go along." All the time the real you is shrieking out, "Just say no!"

We can still be caring people without becoming caretakers!

◆

A weary and worn pastor's wife, overrun with responsibilities, was the last one left after the church service with me. She offered to drive me all the way to my hotel (what else could she do?).

"Sorry," I said, "I didn't mean for you to get drafted into this job."

"Oh," she said with an uncertain sigh, "it's always a pleasure to serve." And she ushered me into her car.

"No," I remarked, buckling my seat belt. "I don't buy it. It's not 'always a pleasure to serve.' Sometimes it's a total bother, a lot of hard work, and nothing but the pits!"

Somehow, my honest response shocked her into reality, and she leaned over the steering wheel sobbing. She began to pour out her overloaded heart to me.

We won't ever get perfect at this self-expression thing, but we can improve and feel proud of ourselves for having the courage of our convictions. Why don't you join me in making some new commitments to openly express ourselves at some upcoming occasions:

> At the next family gathering (ugh!)
> At the next church meeting
> At the next political discussion
> The next time family values are discussed
> The next time . . . (You decide this one!)

You can begin by taking baby steps when you're in a social setting. How about trying this the next time you eat out with a few friends? The waitress approaches the table. You've been perusing the menu, you know you're hungry—your tummy is roaring. As you peer over the top of the menu, you will no doubt hear size 5 friend remark, "I'll have the chicken salad. Hold the bacon and hold the dressing. And could you bring some artificial sweetener for my iced tea?"

A second will remark, "I'd like a side salad and dry wheat toast. Do you have any grapefruit juice?"

A third (skinny) friend will no doubt fall in line with, "I'll have the fish—it's not fried, is it? With the vegetables— no cheese sauce, of course."

Now the heat's on you! Don't cave in! Just tell the waitress, "I'm real hungry. Would you bring the dessert tray first, please?"

Wife, Submit Yourself !

In dealing with a spouse, you have the biblical direction to submit your true self to your husband—including what you feel, think, need, desire, and so on. Expressing yourself—reaching into the depths of you for feelings and pulling them out into the light—is actually a way of submitting yourself to your spouse.

Remember what happened with Janet and Brian and going to the movies? Although the wife did not wind up going to the movie theater with her husband, she did submit her*self* fully to him. She informed him about what was going on inside her, and she unveiled to him her real feelings.

Husband Brian may or may not be happy with the new arrangement. He married a sweet, quiet, inexpressive gal, and now he's watching her change into an expressive, assertive woman. He has his own adjustments to make.

My husband, Hal, and I are putting this principle into action on a weekly basis. Who he is versus who I am is not mutually exclusive, even though we are worlds-apart opposites. Each of us considers it a duty to respect the feelings of the other and to encourage expression—whether it's what we want to hear or not.

I wouldn't call myself an independent woman. I would call myself an *un*dependent woman, enjoying my marriage to a very good man. My husband and I share the kind of life that is rich in collaboration and mutual enjoyment on many levels. We are both autonomous individuals with our own careers who have made the healthy choice to be committed to marriage.

I think we have come to our present understanding because of the extent to which each of us travels and the many periods of separation we experience. I no longer practice what one woman termed "window sitting"— where I longingly wait for him to come home so I can resume my life. This is not, by the way, to say we don't enjoy our times together. On the contrary, our separations make us cherish our shared times even more.

Does "Express Yourself" Mean "Let 'er Rip"?

I hope you won't interpret all this "express yourself" business as a license to walk all over people, starting with those closest to you. It doesn't include the right to say, "I don't like you," or "I think you're all wet," or to participate in the time-tested practice of name-calling: "How can you be such a slob?" or "I should never have married such a lowlife!" You are responsible to consider whether or not you are trying to be downright offensive, to vent your rage, or simply to express your heartfelt desires.

For instance, I love classical music in my home. If I had my way, I'd have it on LOUD, with the rush of violins and the roar of the timpani resounding through every room of the house. Now this definitely wouldn't fly at my home; I'm the only one who likes that "junk." So now the ball is in my court. I can choose to say, "Well, jerks like you don't recognize fine music when you hear it," or I can choose to play it my way when I am alone.

In risking an expression of your true feelings, it is wise to do so in consideration of the person with whom you want to improve your relationship. Your goal is to somehow enhance that association, not to purposely erode it. You don't have permission to shove your opinion down anyone's throat or to intentionally hurt him or her. And punishing people with harsh words can easily escalate into an angry, ongoing quarrel.

Janet said no to the movie in a nice way. She could well have put it: "Look, dummy, you are so hard-hearted and thick-skinned that watching all that violence and filth appeals to you. Go ahead, buddy, get your kicks."

I think Janet chose the more excellent way. The end result was peaceable and as pleasant as possible.

In your closest relationships you're going to have to negotiate your way through the inevitable changes that occur when the real you is emerging. Negotiation means finding a compromise or looking for a middle ground.

- "You always want to eat out and I want to watch the budget. Can we try a fast-food place?"
- "You usually want to watch the late show and I would rather read in bed. Can we keep the TV watching in the TV room?"
- "You like to keep changing channels on the radio, so just when I start getting into a song, it's gone. Could we just listen to a music tape?"
- "You always expect me to drive to your house, but you don't have time to drive here. Could we meet at a restaurant halfway?"
- "You say you want me to be on time to pick you up after rehearsal, and yet when I get there on time, you're

always late. Let's just agree that I'll pick you up fifteen minutes after the rehearsal is over every week."

As you open up to being more authentic in your communication, God will give you the grace to express yourself properly. Inside of you, where the Spirit of Christ lives, He is silently rejoicing, knowing that as you become more transparent, the image of Christ will be more easily seen in you.

Scripture says, "God . . . has given us this ministry of reconciliation." Did it ever occur to you that reconciliation might involve bringing people back to the harmony they desire with their true selves? I think that's part of the process. I suggest you start today—begin by getting better acquainted with the real you. "Seek and ye shall find."

Step No. 5: Reflect Your Redeemer

Let the beauty of the LORD our God be upon us.

Psalm 90:17

What a beautiful word in the Bible: *let!* In the process of performing miracles on our behalf, God allows us to participate by using the word *let* for releasing so many blessings. This word implies several things:

> To share
> To concede
> To permit
> To allow
> To give opportunity
> To free from confinement
> To release

God will permit us to have a hand in opening up our spirits to let/allow His life flow through. We do this by becoming more open, more real. By risking frankness and vulnerability, we are consciously letting Him expand our horizons and live through us more obviously.

God invites our participation in reflecting our Redeemer. John the Baptist stated, "He must increase, and I must decrease." We, too, must decrease in our pretenses and in our defense mechanisms. We can choose to stop defending our images and the focus on ourselves. The choice is up to us.

The sign on my doctor's waiting room wall says it all:

There is nothing the doctor can do which will overcome what the patient WILL NOT DO.

◆

Even the Great Physician cannot overcome what we, the patients, refuse to do. We must choose to let His reflection be greater than our own.

The See-Through Christian

There may be a bit of personal risk and trauma in transparency, but the rewards are well worth the challenges. To be transparent means . . .

to open our hearts.
to be frank.
to exhibit guilelessness.
to be easily detected or seen through, to be obvious.
to be readily understood and clear.
to be honest, unpretentious, and approachable.

When we come to the place of feeling more satisfied with whoever it is that God created us to be, we'll be willing to risk revealing that person to others. This is what I mean when I say "living inside out." We're aware that He has made us well, but we also understand that we are only a container, housing a precious cargo:

> But we have this treasure in earthen vessels, that the excel-
> lence of the power may be of God and not of us (2 Cor. 4:7).

The precious reflection of the real Jesus Christ can be detected only through a transparent housing, through a genuinely crystalline vessel.

Our goal is authenticity: to be the same on the <u>out</u>side as we are on the <u>in</u>side.

◆

To press toward this mark of transparency, we're going to have to "put *off* the old [wo]man, and put *on* the new [wo]man." And the life of this real woman is hidden with Christ, in God. People will recognize that only when she becomes real, transparent herself.

Once our lives on planet Earth are over, we have a better, more satisfying self to look forward to. We will be more like the real Jesus.

> Yes, dear friends, we are already God's children, right now,
> and we can't even imagine what it is going to be like later
> on. But we do know this, that when he comes we will be
> like him, as a result of seeing him as he really is
> (1 John 3:2 TLB).

The Unlikely Candidate

Until we see Jesus face-to-face, our job is to continue becoming the real us, so that we can reflect Him as we work in His service. Let me give you a personal example. For some years I fought off the idea that I could ever be a Christian speaker. No way did I fit the mold, at least not the one I'd seen. I'd sat under many female lecturers, Bible teachers, and preachers, and a number of them made me nervous, feeling worse after the meeting than I did before. Each one seemed to have it all together, and they made me all too aware that I did not.

After considering them, I naturally figured with all the mistakes I'd made in life, I'd never qualify. I struggled to interpret God in the things He allowed in my life. I knew my marriage was made in heaven, but so are thunder and lightning. My kids were not perfect. My humor was a bit warped—I had never heard a Christian woman speaker crack the kind of jokes I did naturally. My poor background, lack of theological credentials, and limited educational opportunities all seemed to spell out D-I-S-Q-U-A-L-I-F-I-E-D.

Our struggles _qualify_ us for service; they make us more compassionate and less judgmental.

◆

I never could have guessed how much women wanted to hear from a woman who was willing to confess that she did *not* have her ducks in a row, and she had lots of unanswered questions herself. How could I have known that confessing my weaknesses and challenges could honestly bring hope to others?

Your inadequacy may be your number <u>one</u> qualification!

◆

Genteel Living

I recall one particular night when I spoke in Dallas. For some reason or other (probably due to the very responsive audience), I was loose as a goose. I had a grand old time, opening up women's hearts with humor so I could slip the truth in. Afterward, a sweet, demure gal shyly slipped me a handwritten note. Here's what she wrote:

> All my life, Lee, my parents taught me what it was to be a poised and genteel southern lady. There seems to be a certain prescribed way to walk and talk for us. No proper Christian lady violates this unspoken code. But then tonight I saw you! [I almost stopped reading.] Thanks, Lee, for breaking the mold, and showing me that God can use anyone who is authentic and transparent. Now I'm sure that God can use me, just as I am— without pretense or imitation. Thanks for the freedom; I'll cherish it!

Nowadays I speak all over the world, and wherever I go, I've been surprised to see how even a rigid, legalistic church group will genuinely respond to my attempt to be honest and open. It's easier for me to speak if I bare my soul and unveil my weaknesses. And the remark I hear more than any one single comment is, "You were so *real*! Thanks."

The Light Down Under

One particular individual's response stands out in my mind. He had been assigned to me, this Australian pastor. His senior pastor had asked him to be my host, and so he had to be proper and civil, whether he liked it or not. He was soft-spoken (not unlike many there), and I was aware of him quietly observing me throughout the days I spoke in different settings in his area. This fellow was no laid-back Crocodile Dundee. He seemed leery of me, always "discerning" me.

As he drove me to the airport, he unexpectedly asked me, " 'ow did you get it, mate?"

"How did I get what?"

" 'ow did you get so free? I've had my eye on you. I wasn't sure I liked you at first. You were so different from the other Bible teachers we'd had come through here. You don't get your knickers in a knot."

"I don't get my what?"

"You know, you don't get all uptight. You've got a sincere heart, but you don't act as holy as I expected you to. You knew you were different, but you didn't seem to mind they were wonderin' if you were two snags short of a Barbie. And you knew the people took awhile to get used to you, especially with that Yankee accent o' yours and all, but you didn't change any to suit them."

"Honestly, I fought off the impulse to change and try harder to fit in," I admitted. "I could tell their resistance was up because I told some jokes and acted a bit zany at times. I could tell you are not used to that in your churches."

"Bug on, mate!" he chuckled. "You're sort of a Mrs. Benny Hill character if you know what I mean. But you won them over—the whole kit and caboodle of 'em—in spite of it all because you was true blue *real*, I guess you could say."

I could see that he was catching on, so I went a little further. "I've learned transparency is a big part of my relationship with God and others because if I have the channel between Him and me stuffed up with pride or self-consciousness, my lifeline is cut off. I'm the only one He's given me, and I've got to be faithful in the little He has given me, so I can grow."

The man seemed to take courage. "You know, you wouldn't have guessed it from being with me, but I've got a bit of a sense of humor myself! [He was right; I never would have guessed it.] But I never thought it was, well, proper to use it in the pulpit."

"Which one is the *real you*? The one with the sense of humor, or the one without?" I inquired. "God will accept no substitutes—nothing artificial added, and nothing natural taken away, either. It might cost you a bit at first, but your people will be even more pleased when they see *you* emerge!"

He smiled a Cheshire-cat smile and stammered, "You know, I think this bloke's got it, too!"

"Great! Hold on to it, and don't let the Pharisees steal it from you—or put you in jail over it!" As we parted, he had tears in his eyes. He said he thought he'd never be the same again. As I left, I felt as if I'd left a little piece of my heart in that lovely country "down under."

Physical Jesus

The earthly family of Jesus did not see the real Him. For all intents and purposes, He appeared to be a good boy who was learning His father's carpentry business. After all, He was Joseph's eldest son, wasn't He?

In fact, Jesus was a young man of questionable legitimacy. The rumor had surely traveled that Mary had been pregnant with Him before she'd married Joseph. John 7:5 informs us that even the brothers of Jesus "did not believe in Him."

Even the greatness of His miracles provided only a peek at the real Jesus. He calmed the sea; but He had been there when the earth was first separated from the waters. He walked on the water; but the real Jesus had created the ocean currents. He healed the sick and raised the dead; but the real Jesus, whose true identity was hidden behind His flesh costume, had participated in creating life at the beginning of time.

> Let this mind be in you which was also in Christ Jesus, who, being in the form of God, did not consider it robbery to be equal with God, but made Himself of no reputation, taking the form of a bondservant, and coming in the likeness of men. And being found in appearance as a man, He humbled Himself and became

obedient to the point of death, even the death of the
cross (Phil. 2:5-8).

Jesus may have been hiding His glory behind a veil of
humanity, but He was always real—demonstrating plainly
who He was regardless of the consequences. He made no
compromises. And as supreme a being as He truly was, He
chose to let Himself be vulnerable.

The Accessible Christ

The Lord Jesus could easily grab a towel and wash His
disciples' feet. Because Jesus knew who He was, He could
feel comfortable in any task that needed doing.

Jesus could risk being ridiculed—even stoned—by
folks who did not recognize His identity. Yet that very
vulnerability endeared Him to the sincere seekers. He had
no fear of being exposed. In her book *Women Reveal What
They Fear Most*, author Carol Kent talks about the unre-
vealed Christ:

> People were always bringing hurting friends to Jesus.
> What was it about this man that made Him so approach-
> able? Everywhere Jesus went He did two things: "He
> looked at him (her) with compassion," and "He touched
> them."
> What a practical example Christ is for us! He never
> minced words; He never skirted the issues. To the Phari-
> sees, He remarked, "You are of your father, the devil."
> Now there's a way to endear yourself to a group of influ-
> ential people! To the adulterous woman, He said, "Go
> your way, and sin no more." He did not pretend to ad-
> mire the woman, but neither did He condemn her.

Those who understood gained respect for Jesus because
He was real!

Our Example: The Unveiled Christ

Let's look at it another way. Have you ever considered
this? On the earth, Jesus Christ was masked. He appeared
to be the "lowly man from Galilee" masked under "the form
of a bondservant," as Paul noted in Philippians 2. He dressed
Himself in human flesh. But that was not the real Jesus.

Philippians 2 says that Jesus Christ Himself was cov-
ered, and that He took on Himself the form of a servant
and was made in the likeness of men. He became a man so
He could take our place. It was not until His resurrection
that the real Christ became apparent; His veil was lifted.
Hebrews 10:20 says Christ paved a new and living way for
us, "through the veil, that is, His flesh."

In His dying for us on the cross, immediately the veil
in the Jewish temple was ripped—from the top to the
bottom, revealing the Holiest of Holies that was hidden
behind it. And the same happened with the real Christ when
His flesh was torn. When He died, He unveiled Himself,
and the power of resurrection took over, revealing the real
Christ. He was no gentle, meek, and mild human being;
He was the original Perfect Being, the only begotten Son
of the living God.

His powerful reality was soon obvious to all.

In His resurrection, the real Christ became Himself, a
reflection of the true God. We are to reflect His radiance
by becoming clear glass. Prisms receive the invisible light
of the sun and send out all the beautiful colors of the

rainbow. So we are to reflect God's light, displaying to our world all the colorful attributes of our God. Let our unveiling begin.

> But we all, with unveiled face, beholding as in a mirror the glory of the Lord, are being transformed into the same image (2 Cor. 3:18.)

Reflections of Joy

You have as much laughter as you have faith!
Martin Luther

How are we to reflect God's glory? Martin Luther had the right idea! Humor demonstrates the joy of the Lord. And I believe it becomes easier to see the humor in life as we combine it with our faith. Before I entered into the Christian walk, I believed I'd have to put aside my sense of humor to be a serious person of faith. But quite the contrary is true! Now it is easier for me to see the positive side of a negative happening.

Running out of gas (especially on a Los Angeles freeway!) can be a real bummer, but my faith tells me God can make something good out of it—maybe I'll meet an angel who'll help me out.

Getting the flu is never fun, but I realize it's a great excuse to stay home and catch up on my reading.

I may not enjoy sitting through boring lectures, but it helps me figure out what I'm *not* going to do or say the next time I'm in front of an audience!

Jesus must have had a sense of humor to deal with the men He had to work with. They wouldn't have been

considered the cream of the crop by today's standards—
not your average rocket scientists. So often the disciples
didn't understand the Master; they misinterpreted a lot
of things. Truly God uses the foolish things to confound
the wise. God will use the foolish things about us, mix
them up with joy spilling forth from faith, to make us a
more lighthearted, pleasant people. The joy of the Lord
is a strength to us.

Joy is the most infallible sign of the presence of God.

◆

Soul-Searching

In church we sing the hymn with gusto: "Awake my
soul! Stretch every nerve." I wonder if our souls may still
be sleeping? Can you describe for me the difference between your *soul* and your *spirit*? Don't just think in psychological terms, regarding the definitions of *mind, will,* and
emotions. What is the difference in practical terms?

I believe we have actually lost touch with our souls—the
inner residence of the real us. In popular Christian thought the
soul is simply something to be saved. A soul is for converting,
not communing—that is too mystical, too subjective, too . . .
you know . . . New Age-ish. The church shies away from
dealing with matters of the soul after conversion.

Wittenburg Door magazine editor Mike Yaconelli got
me considering all this when he wrote,

We have lost touch with our souls. We have been nour-
ishing our minds, our relational skills, our theological
knowledge, our psychological well-being, our physi-
ological health, but we've abandoned our souls. Our
souls have been lost.

I think that's pretty accurate when we consider how
well we've learned what the accepted Christian pattern is:
how we should appear, act, and think. But that conformity
has not brought unity or maturity to the body of Christ. It
has not helped to liberate our individuality or enhanced the
expression of our gifts from the Spirit.

When you are consumed by the external and by
the demands of everyday life, you cease doing soul
work. One day you wake up virtually soulless. You find
yourself busy, superficial, and friendless. And Jesus was
warning us in Mark 8:36 by saying, "What will it profit
a man if he gains the whole world, and loses his own
soul?"

Reexamining the authenticity with which we express
what is going on in our souls is healthy living. Checking
ourselves for cover-ups, pretenses, and the like can lead
only to a more genuine expression of who God created us
to be.

Long lay the world, in sin and error pining—'till *He* appeared, and the soul felt its worth!

Let's concentrate on the process of what the psalmist
said the Shepherd would do for us: "He restoreth my soul."

Conforming to What Image?

Sometimes, too, we're faced with a lost soul in someone close to us. One discouraged wife, glancing at her husband's picture, sighed, "I will always treasure the false image I had of you." Do we have false images of ourselves? Of those we love? Maybe in the past we've tried to conform our images to match someone else's idea.

"Do not be conformed to this world, but be transformed by the renewing of your mind," advises Paul in Romans 12:2. Our goal—our destiny—in life is to shoot that nonconforming target.

AIM: To be conformed to the image of Christ.

◆

Romans 8:29 shows us God's motivation:

> For those whom He foreknew, He also predestined to
> be conformed to the image of His Son, that He [Jesus]
> might be the firstborn among many brethren.

God desires that we begin to adapt and adjust ourselves to resemble only one person in thought and behavior: Jesus Christ. When we seek to be conformed to His image, we are touching on God's ultimate desire for us. God would like to have many children who all behave like the Son who gave His life for us.

Jesus planted Himself, like a seed, in earth to sprout and bring forth multiplied millions of others with the potential to be like Him. There is no one else we are to imitate or conform to. We are not permitted to fashion ourselves into any image we choose. We are to follow the Master's plan.

Are we ready to lose our lives for Christ's sake, giving up all our pretense and learned behavior? Let's surrender all these man-made people-pleasing and fitting-in patterns. When we sacrifice them, from their ashes will emerge an unfettered spirit, unencumbered by pretense and veneer. If the plan of God for our lives was designed around the real us, we don't want to miss out—for Christ's sake or for our own sakes.

Feel Like Yourself!

My business is not to remake myself, but to make the absolute best of what God made.

Robert Browning

Are you making the best of the real you? Remember to concentrate on stripping, not striving, and the originality of who you are will soon be clearly visible. You are seeking to recover your original design, and it will be unique!

Think of yourself as an original work of art. If you want to be an original, you've got to be different.

◆

Let's make a quick review of the things we've learned about reclaiming our real selves. Thanks be to God, there is no earthly image to which we are to conform—no one else we are supposed to imitate to please God. There is no approved stereotype or prototype for a real child of God. So while God radically transforms you in Christ, you find that you are becoming more yourself than you ever were before. Here's why He is so concerned about your authenticity:

You are the best person to do what God has called you to do!

◆

Reaching for Your Goal

The goal at the end of reclaiming the real you is not self-realization. Your aim is far beyond that. To know yourself is good, but to realize Christ can be more fully Himself in you—*that* is the challenge. Far more than some humanistic New Age approach to self-image, the Christian's goal, through authenticity, is transparency.

Christ's goal for you, as Psalm 23 records, is this: "He restores my soul." The Lord is in the position of being the Restorer of the breach between your original creation and the individual you appear to be today. When that restoration is complete, you will realize your full potential.

When we begin our self-examination work, the Great Physician will begin His work— from the inside out!

◆

Your Buried Treasure

When Jesus told the parable about the unfaithful steward who hid his treasure and later lost it, He was talking

to each of us. If we continue to hide our real selves, we run
the risk of losing our identity forever. Don't bury yourself!
Be faithful in what is your own. There is no one waiting in
the wings to be you in this life; you have no understudy to
take your place if you blow it. The world needs the real
you.

If you won't be you, who will? If not now, when?

◆

Jesus told another parable about a man stumbling over
buried treasure in an untended field. This parable encourages us to sell all and sell out to go hunting for that treasure.
I believe the treasure we hold inside us—the precious life
of Christ—is waiting to be claimed, recognized, and un-
earthed.

Faith doesn't teach us how to move moun-tains; it teaches us how to climb or tunnel through them!

◆

Reach Out and Touch the Real You

We've already talked about the little child's chair
from the garage sale and the many coats of paint that hid
its real beauty and value from the world. Like that chair,
you are ready to submit yourself to the Carpenter's stripping
process.

Step No. 1: Receive the Truth

The truth about why you're alive goes beyond the fact that your mom and dad made love. God made your life. You were His decision. He wanted the unique you to exist. Sin damaged that life He made, and Jesus (the living Truth) paid the price of your restoration to life with God. Receive the One who is truth—He can set you free.

Step No. 2: Remove the Layers

Realize that God created something good when He made you. He will give you the courage to begin your unpeeling process. All of us have some veneers behind which we are hidden—self-protective coatings behind which we are camouflaged. Reclaiming your real self means committing yourself to the task of stripping off those pretenses. It also involves using the veneer stripper of forgiveness, which you have in your emotional closet, with which you can begin to dissolve the heavy layers that burden you. Jesus is calling, "Come to Me, all you who labor and are heavy laden."

Step No. 3: Review the Present

Taking healthy inventory of your present involvements is so helpful in answering the question: Am I being real? Take a long look at your emotions, your fears, and your relationships. Are you trying to fit in to be accepted? Are you conforming to try to receive love from a person or a group? An inventory of your present lifestyle can help you see what needs to be changed and what doesn't.

An original will try to adapt the world to herself; a copy will try to adapt herself to the world.

◆

> Don't copy the behavior and customs of this world, but be a new and different person with a fresh newness in all you do and think. Then you will learn from your own experience how his ways will really satisfy you (Rom. 12:2 TLB).

Step No. 4: Risk Revealing the Real You

What a sense of freedom comes when you let go of false pretenses and risk being real! If you are honest, you'll begin redrawing the boundary lines that have been blurred. Only be a caretaker over the things that really matter in life; the other things you can simply care for if you wish. Risk communicating who you truly are—what you think and want and need. Risk living on the edge— revealing your true self. Provide things *honest* "in the sight of all men" (Rom. 12:17).

Step No. 5: Reflect Your Redeemer

Allow Christ to be revealed through your newfound authenticity. You can hope to be a reflection of Him only by becoming transparent—clearly and unmistakably real. Permitting the resurrection power of Jesus to have rule over you will make your veil disappear. Your soul will then be restored as you cry with the hymnist, "Oh, to be like Thee, blessed Redeemer!"

Enjoy the Unveiling

Does all this really make a difference? I've heard wonderful reports from scores of women who have finally discovered their real selves. But I can speak best for myself. I am greatly enjoying discovering the woman God meant for me to be. I am more relaxed in my work, giving myself wholeheartedly and unreservedly to the ministry He has given me. I'm risking both publicly and privately now. In my family, I am more at ease in dealing with conflict, trusting that as I am transparent and honest about who I am, the peace of Christ will help me solve my problems.

Spiritually, I am more at rest than I've ever been. Although I used to depend on the better judgment of anyone else over my own, now I'm trying to completely trust God's leading within me. I've learned to enjoy what it means to stand fast in the liberty that Christ has given to me. No, I still don't have all the answers, but I can relate to 2 Chronicles 20:12: "Nor do we know what to do, but our eyes are upon You"! As I trust in the Lord, I find Him more influential within me. Whenever I see this sign, it reminds me where to look:

Help Wanted: Inquire Within

◆

Like you, I realize that God is not finished with me yet. No, I haven't attained yet. I'm not in the major leagues yet, but I'm practicing for them. I can relate to what one grand Christian writer penned:

Think of me as a fellow-patient in the same hospital who, having been admitted a little earlier, could give some advice.

C. S. Lewis

One of my goals in life, as warped as it might sound, is to become a sweet old lady. I don't know a whole lot of them, do you? When I'm old and gray (or should I say older and grayer?), I want to be able to sit in my rocking chair on the porch, enjoying life, savoring who I've become in life, and being grateful for all God has done. In those sunset years, I want to be able to sigh along with the composer of the beloved hymn, "It is well with my soul"!

Feeling a Bit Unqualified?

A feeling of inadequacy may be your first qualification for usefulness by the Master. Do you feel . . .

too simple? *He chooses the foolish things of the world to confound the wise (see 1 Cor. 1:27).*
too young? *Except you become as a little child, you cannot enter the kingdom of God (see Mark 10:15).*
not smart enough? *Not many wise, not many noble, are called (see 1 Cor. 1:26).*
immature? *He hides things from the wise and reveals them to babes (see Matt. 11:25).*

not healed in body, mind, or spirit? *The Great Physician came for the sick (see Mark 2:17).*

God doesn't want your ability. He wants your availability!

◆

Whatever Happened to the Spirit of God?

Nothing! This Holy Spirit is the presence of Christ within us; Jesus promised to send another Comforter, and He came special delivery when we asked forgiveness for sins and invited Him into our lives. Since He is also referred to as the Spirit of truth (John 14:17), He wants us to peel down to the truthful, original creation.

> We have received . . . the Spirit who is from God, that we might know the things that have been freely given to us by God (1 Cor. 2:12).

When Jesus spoke about the Holy Spirit, He said, "He will teach you all things" (John 14:26). That makes my mouth water! The more room we make in our lives for this Spirit of truth, the more the revealing, penetrating light of God will shine through us. Living out the true life of Christ in us—the real us—is our only hope of glory!

I haven't found any other source of well-being outside a living relationship with Christ. No psychological Band-Aid, emotional catharsis, or intellectual debate has the power to enable us to discover who and why God created us the way He did—the real us. Then, after having done all, we can stand—allow the Real Us to stand up!

We could chime in with Peter, as he answered Jesus, saying,

> Lord, to whom shall we go? You have the words of eternal life (John 6:68).

Colossians 3:10 (converted to the female gender) says,

> Put on the new woman who is renewed in knowledge according to the image of Him who created her.

Let Your Light Shine

As you become more and more transparent, Christ has an opportunity to become more apparent in you. Instead of folks looking on your outward appearance, they'll be more struck with what they find so evident inside. The love of God endures forever for the real you, to restore, to renew, to redeem and refinish that person He always meant you to be.

You are a unique creation, fashioned by a great Carpenter who always had you in mind. He wants you to openly and unashamedly display what He has made in you—your unique pattern that He compares to no one else on this planet.

Think of yourself as being assigned the job of general contractor for rebuilding the real you. Your raw materials are provided; you've had a glimpse of the schematic. He has given you the skills necessary to begin that refinishing process. Remember:

What you are is God's gift to you; what you do with what you are is your gift to God.

◆